Recommendations

Dr. Jim Croley's book, *The Blinding of America*, is the result of an inspired idea. He has used his knowledge and experience as an eye surgeon to enlighten us to the dangers of today's new technologies. The American culture has lost its way and his book proves the case that America is in danger, not from without but from within. The new ideologies of the progressives has run amok. Dr. Croley's book is not only a Christian call to arms, but a training manual for preparing to fight this cultural war.

> — Dale M. Hayden, *City Director*,
> The C.S. Lewis Institute – Naples, FL

Dr. Croley has written a very insightful book on a topic of great importance today, especially for our young people. With so much visual stimulation being ubiquitous in our culture it is easy to underestimate how much we are impacted by all that we see. Supported by expert scientific analysis, lessons from history and Biblical truth, Dr. Croley has given us an important message for our time. This book will inspire soul-searching as to our beliefs, our worldview and vision of reality. With such clear and engaging writing, you will not want to put this book down. It is a page-turner!

> — Dr. Steven Michael Grant,
> *Pastor*

Dr. Croley leads us on a fascinating journey through the world of sight in all its dimensions. The many parallels between physical eyesight (which enables our brains to process the material world) and spiritual vision (which enables our true inner selves to understand God and life's moral choices) are remarkable and memorable. Every Christian will benefit from these insights. They bring us both warning and encouragement. After helping thousands of patients to see the world better, this renowned eye surgeon is now correcting our spiritual vision!

— Dr. Doug Pratt, *Senior Pastor*
First Presbyterian of Bonita Springs

This book will "open your eyes" to the gradual and deliberate darkness that is descending over our culture. Jim Croley writes with the precise insight of a trained ophthalmologist and the pure vision of a committed Christian. Every page is filled with lines that call you to pause—in wonder, in alarm, or in sober reflection. Reading this book is corrective *cataract surgery* for the mind's eye.

— Allen Walworth
Executive Vice President
Generis

Table of Contents

Introduction

The Holy Spirit put the thought in my mind that I needed to write a second book. I thought I was finished with writing books. Evidently, God thinks that as an ophthalmologist and Christian, I can provide unique information about living a Christian life. The thought the Holy Spirit gave me was that virtually all sin that man commits comes initially through our vision. Temptation comes to you through your vision. Your first exposure to sin is through your vision. Afterward, other parts of your brain will contribute to your response to the temptation. So, it would be best if you were very careful about what you look at or be cautious about things that attract your attention.

Many things in this world, in your life, or in the environment are obviously sinful, such as pornography. Other sins or manipulations of our mind may not be so apparent. The secular world and Satan are aggressively trying to change how you think, believe, and act. Most of the time, you are tempted or influenced in tiny and subtle ways. There are 85 references in the Bible about the deception of Satan, such as being a wolf in sheep's clothing. There are many Bible verses about Satan as the great deceiver. One verse is 2 Corinthians 11:14 NLT.

But I am not surprised!
Even Satan disguises himself
as an angel of light.

One morning after I had finished the book, I woke up at 4:00 a.m. with the thought that I needed to change the title of the book. God wanted me to take the book further into the deception vision can have in your life.

What has happened to America? Families have been torn apart, as younger Americans no longer believe in God and hate America's current culture and society. Thanksgiving dinners can no longer be enjoyed as a family. Christmas is only a commercial event in December. America has lost its way or has left the morals, principles, and ethics that formed the foundation of American life. Many Americans have been blinded to the core of its foundation. Like many of the other powerful nations in the past, America is crumbling from within. No superpower nation is causing its demise. The fabric of America has been bleached of its heritage from within its borders.

America was founded on Judeo-Christian principles. The form of our government and our laws were based on Christian laws and beliefs. A radical group of people, organizations, companies, and left-wing radical government officials are viciously destroying America. God is being removed from our society. America needs to acquire pure vision, perfect perception, and the ultimate reality of God's sovereignty.

The people of America and the Western World are being blinded by Big Tech, radical leftist people and groups, the national news media, and radical leftists in government. They realize that what you see on television or flat screens daily is who you become. Your paradigm is composed of all the things and events you observe. These people believe that their form of Marxism is the ultimate utopia. In their beliefs, everyone will be treated in a fair and equal manner. No one is better than another—and everyone should live life in the same way or condition. These people are clueless. It sounds great, but that is not how real life plays out. Everyone has different talents and abilities. We are all unique. There is equal opportunity for everyone, but not identical outcomes. Everyone should not get a trophy just for participating.

Every Marxist country has been a failure and has killed in the neighborhood of 100 million people in the 20th century. The bloodiest century of humankind was at the hands of Marxist regimes, such as Joseph Stalin in the Soviet Union, Khmer Rouge in Cambodia, Mao in China, and Hitler in Germany. These radical people, groups, and corporations have been blinded to reality. People, looking for a way of life where everyone is treated equally, should turn to God. He loves everyone and wants a relationship with every person. Christians are to love their neighbors, as they love themselves. That is the way we are to live life.

The information fed into most flat screens is designed to brainwash you into believing what they want you to believe. The national news programs reported on the riots in the year 2020. The reporter is standing in front of a scene of burning buildings and people looting businesses, while telling you the riots are actually peaceful protests. They believe they have blinded you to reality and you do not see the chaos behind them. They want to remove freedom and God from American society. The propaganda on all flat screens is continuous. Everyone is addicted to watching and are controlled and manipulated by these radical people.

The television programs of today would have been censored a generation earlier. Big Tech controls all your searches on the internet, so they can control the things you see. They follow all your searches as well and have developed a profile about you. The government wants to tell you what kind of car to drive, how to control the thermostat in your home, and what you can eat. Every commercial on TV tells you their product is the best. Flat screens are influencing every aspect of living. Life is beginning to look like some of the sci-fi movies of life in the future, where the collective controls everything. God will be banned from life on earth.

The blind are never unperceptive
but the unperceptive are always blind.

— Randi G. Fine

So, I decided to write this book to show you how Satan and his followers are trying to change you and society and how you can detect their schemes. The radical left wants you blinded, as to their goals and tactics. Let's take the veil off your eyes and begin our journey into looking at pure vision, perfect perception, and ultimate reality, by looking at the first story in humankind's history.

Sin came into humans in the very beginning. Humankind's vision got us in trouble very early on. In the beginning, God created a wondrous and beautiful world. If you take the time to observe the universe purposefully, it will amaze you. God designed everything in the universe, even the smallest things known, such as quarks and leptons. These tiny particles are 24 million times smaller than a grain of sand. God made the most massive star in the universe, CV Canis Majoris, which is 1,500 times larger than our Sun. It would occupy the space from our Sun to the orbit of Saturn around the Sun. It is beyond our imagination to conceive of a single star that massive, 40,000 degrees Fahrenheit—and God just breathed it into existence! The human mind is unable to comprehend the power and majesty of God.

God planted a majestic garden in Eden. It was full of beautiful plants and trees. Many of the trees produced delicious fruit. God placed the tree of life and the knowledge of good and evil in the middle of His garden. God placed man in the garden to tend and watch over His creation. He created Eve to be man's companion. God told Adam and Eve that they might freely eat from every tree in the garden, except from the tree of good and evil knowledge. If they ate its fruit, they would surely to die.

This tree must have been something special, as it was in the center of the Garden of Eden. Is there a reason that it was in the center of the Garden of Eden? That tree contained the future of humanity. Genesis 3:6 says that the tree was beautiful and its fruit looked delicious. How powerfully vision influences us is found at the beginning of Genesis. I am guessing, but maybe it was the most beautiful tree in the Garden, as God placed it in the center of His marvelous creation. Do you think the fruit might have been the most beautiful of all the fruits on the garden trees? And maybe it had the best-tasting fruit in the garden!

What about the serpent? The Bible describes the serpent as shrewd, cunning, subtle, and the craftiest of all the wild animals that God created. Maybe that is one of the reasons Satan decided to enter into the serpent. The character of the serpent fits what Satan wanted to accomplish. Satan could have entered a bunny rabbit instead. But do you think he would have gotten the same result as a cute little bunny rabbit? Using the serpent, he stimulated the emotional portion of Eve's brain, the limbic system. Many people are extremely fearful of snakes. Satan knew the sight of the serpent would weaken Eve's decision-making area of her brain. When the emotional part of your brain is stimulated, the activity in the rational part of your brain is diminished. You make poor decisions when under stress or when emotionally upset! Through the serpent, Satan stimulated Eve's emotional state. Therefore she was less capable of making a rational decision. Satan is an expert at deception and manipulation!

If the tree was an ugly, straggly looking tree and the fruit smelled and looked unappealing, Eve may not have made that horrible decision. I believe that Satan picked the best fruit from the tree. Maybe he even polished it up a little, just like polishing an apple. (Remember how the witch enticed Sleeping Beauty with a beautifully polished apple). Satan wanted this piece of fruit to be the most enticing fruit in the garden. On top of that, he convinced Eve that it had other unique properties. Satan told her that God had lied to her, that she would be like the all-powerful God of creation, if she ate the fruit.

Genesis 3:5 NLT

God knows that your eyes will be opened
as soon as you eat it,
and you will be like God,
knowing both good and evil.

Satan told her that God wanted to keep all that power to Himself, but that she could be like God, the creator of everything in the universe. That was a pretty enticing proposition! What if the fruit tasted nasty and sour? Maybe Eve would not have offered it to Adam? That would have been an interesting situation.

Research has shown that as much as 90% of communication is visual. Satan used his knowledge to visually entice Eve to commit the sin that would forever change humankind's course. The brain of human beings permanently changed at that moment. The genetic structure of the human brain was altered. The limbic system responsible for all our powerful and negative emotions became a significant component of our actions. Up until this time, there was no record of any negative emotions by Adam or Eve. They were living in paradise and everything was perfect—no stress in their lives. They had no evil or sinful thoughts. The limbic system, and especially the area called the amygdala (where all your strong emotions, such as lust, anger, rage, and fear originate), became activated in a new and compelling manner after eating the fruit. Adam and Eve never experienced these emotions until then. Satan knew this would start the downfall of humankind.

Satan is in charge of this world. He has a large number of fallen angels in his army. God banished him to earth, but also let him have dominion over the earth.

2 Corinthians 4:4 NLT

Satan who is the God of this world,
has blinded the minds of those who don't believe.

Revelation 12:7-9, 12 NLT

Then there was war in heaven. Michael and his angels fought against the dragon and his angel. And the dragon lost the battle, and he and his angels were forced out of heaven. This great dragon—the ancient serpent called the devil, or Satan, the one deceiving the whole world—was thrown down to the earth with all his angels.

Therefore, rejoice, O heavens! And you who live in the heavens, rejoice! But the terror will come down on the

earth and the sea, for the devil has come down to you in
great anger, knowing that he has little time.

Even Jesus acknowledged that Satan is in charge of this world. Luke 4 shows that when Jesus was in the wilderness for forty days, He agreed with Satan's claim that he has dominion over the earth.

Luke 4:5-8 NLT

Then the devil took him up and revealed to him all the
kingdoms of the world in a moment of time. "I will give
you the glory of these kingdoms and authority over them,"
the devil said, "because they are mine to give to anyone
I please. I will give it all to you if you will worship me."
Jesus replied, "The Scriptures say, 'You must worship
your God and serve only him.'"

Jesus did not correct Satan about having the authority to give Jesus all the kingdoms. Instead, Jesus reminded him that all are to worship God and to only serve God.

Satan wasted no time. As soon as God placed Adam in charge of creation, Satan immediately changed the course of life on earth, by enticing Adam and Eve to listen to him and sin against God. Satan and his followers never rest.

As Christians, we need to be diligent in following the guidance of the Holy Spirit. Satan and his followers are always trying to blur your vision, alter your perception, and blind you to reality. Children in America are in greater danger, as they are more addicted to flat screens than adults. People who are not Christians may have difficulty seeing with clear vision, having proper perception, and understanding reality. That is why it is so imperative for you to train your vision to approach what I call **pure vision**, which leads to perfect perception and ultimate reality. Do not let the secular world blind you. Let's get started.

When truth and facts are not seen correctly or simply ignored,
then the propaganda of lies become perceived as facts,
truth, and reality. Even though your eyes can see,
do not be blind!

Chapter 1

Pure Vision

1 Corinthians 13:12 NLT

Now we see things imperfectly, like puzzling reflections in a mirror, but then we will see everything with perfect clarity. All that I know now is partial and incomplete, but then I will know everything completely, just as God knows me completely.

The heart has eyes which the brain knows nothing of.
— Charles H. Parkhurst

What is pure vision? What I am calling pure vision could also be known as spiritual vision. Another way to see this (pun intended) would be to see through the eyes of Jesus. How does Jesus see? Jesus sees everything through pure vision with perfection perception. He knows and has created ultimate reality. He could see everything that was going to happen, before it happened. You and I will never have that type of pure vision, but you can train yourself to see life from a significantly better vantage point. I am not saying that you can train your eyes to have much sharper vision than you do, or that you can obtain vision better than 20/20. Some people do have better than routine normal eyes and can see better than 20/20. When I was younger, I was fortunate to have 20/10 vision,

1

uncorrected without glasses. Realize that seeing with 20/20 vision does not mean you always perceive or understand what your eyes are seeing.

Perception is merely reality filtered
through the prism of your soul.

— Christopher A. Ray

As an ophthalmologist, I feel that vision is the most crucial sense of the five senses! I might go so far as to say that God created man's heart so that the eye would receive blood and oxygen—so you could see! Now I might be stretching this a bit. But our vision so complicated and essential, that the vision center in the brain occupies one of the four lobes of the cerebral cortex. Let us take a more in-depth look at eyes from a historical aspect and their prominence in the Bible. There are many idioms about the eyes. Here are just a few of them.

A twinkle in someone's eye—a bird's eye view—a gleam in someone's eye—an eagle eye—the apple of one's eye—a sight for sore eyes—the eye of the storm—catch someone's eye—beauty is in the eye of the beholder—the eye of the needle—eye-opener— keep an eye on—keep your eye on the ball—keep your eye peeled—in the blink of an eye—see eye to eye—and in the eyes of the law. This is just a small selection. Eyes are everywhere! Even potatoes have eyes!

C.S. Lewis talked about reading literature, saying that it allows us to see with different eyes. The eye played a prominent role in Egyptian mythology and religion. The eye became a metaphor for the sun, the formal cause of creation for the Egyptians. The sun was named the Eye of Re. In ancient Mesopotamia, the term *bright eye* meant a happy face, a *sharp eye* indicated intelligence, and *an evil eye* meant anger or the intention to do wrong.

There are many instances throughout the Bible where knowledge and wisdom are associated with sight. Ignorance and sin are associated with darkness and no sight. Proverbs uses the eye or vision in many verses about describing life.

Proverbs 28:11 NLT

Rich people may think they are wise, but a poor person with discernment can see right through them.

The Scriptures use the eye to describe the moral character and attitude of man.

In Mere Christianity, C.S. Lewis says, "Virtue—even attempted virtue—brings light; indulgence brings fog."

Jeremiah 5:21 NLT

Listen, you foolish and senseless people, with eyes that do not see and ears that do not hear.

Isaiah says the same thing.

Isaiah 44:18 NLT

Such stupidity and ignorance! Their eyes are closed, and they cannot see. Their minds are shut, and they cannot think.

Cicero

*The face is a picture of the mind
with the eyes as its interpreter.*

As I said, the only entity that has pure vision is God. Jesus was able to have pure vision through his human eyes. We need to strive for that same ability to see. It is not just 20/20 vision, but it is much more involved than just reading a chart on a wall in an eye doctor's office. Psalm 94:9 tells us that God sees all. He is omnipotent. God knows all and sees all. God sees not just people's physical appearance, but He sees the innermost thoughts of all people. He created the universe and all the laws of physics that are present in the universe.

As I said at the beginning, I believe that most sin enters your life initially by what you see or observe. In 2 Samuel 11, David's eyes cause him to sin. On a late afternoon, David looked out from his palace rooftop and saw a beautiful woman bathing. That single view of Bathsheba grabbed his attention. The emotional part of his brain or mind was suddenly stimulated. He succumbed to the lust and emotion of desire of the lower levels of his brain function. His eyes caused him to sin.

Do you think that if one of David's guards had told him about a beautiful lady living a few houses away from the palace, King David would have left the palace to look for her? Probably not! It only took a single glimpse of Bathsheba bathing—and he was toast. The limbic area of his brain took control. King David is one of God's favorite people and is known for his love of God. But his lust emitted from his amygdala was so powerful that it led him to murder Uriah the Hittite, Bathsheba's husband.

The limbic system can be the dominating force in many people's lives, if they continually bombard this portion of the brain by observing overstimulating types of things. It is essential that we have a direct connection from our vision to the limbic system for our safety, so that the flight or fight response can be quickly initiated when needed. This is an essential pathway, because if you see something dangerous, you want to respond immediately.

But it has a negative side, as people can let this portion of the brain rule their lives. Unless there is an emergency or something suddenly appears in our environment, we choose the direction we are looking. It is necessary for you to control the things your eyes see.

Later, after David asked God for forgiveness, he realized how his eyes had tempted him. He wrote this in Psalm 101.

Psalm 101:3 NLT

I will refuse to look at anything vile and vulgar.

King David learned through personal experience—what you look at, can get you into trouble. You choose what you look at. Where you look indicates the attitude of your soul. The sin of lust is committed with your eyes. The sin of idolatry is committed with your eyes. Man has made many statues and idols throughout history so that they can look at something to worship. Idols may not be just man-made statues. You can desire or worship driving a fancy car, money, a house, and power. Manufacturers of automobiles run commercials to entice you with their vehicle. They make you think that you would be successful, attract beautiful women, and look fantastic if you are driving their car.

Proverbs 27:20 NIV

Death and destruction are never satisfied,
and neither are human eyes.

Unfortunately, your limbic system (the portion of the brain where all of your strong emotions originate) is always working and ready to lead you astray. The word *flesh* is used in the Bible many times about the desires of the body. The limbic system in the brain is the same as the flesh in the Bible. If you see something dangerous, the limbic system releases chemicals in your body which enable you to respond to the perilous situation physically. So, what your eyes are looking toward, can directly stimulate your limbic system and cause a rush of different emotions and responses. The continuous stimulation of this portion of your brain causes you to become addicted to what you are observing.

The brain develops new brain cells related to everything you observe, study, or experience. As you watch more evil things, the brain will keep producing more brain cells and connections for wherever you are focusing your attention. The brain modifies itself by the information it is receiving. There will be more and more robust pathways in the brain related to sin. It becomes easier to sin. Your life can quickly become hard-wired to the temptations of the secular world. If you spend time looking at vile and vulgar things, you will eventually succumb to that temptation. There is a constant daily battle in the brain between the limbic system with the desire of your strong emotions and the logical portion of the cerebral cortex, especially the prefrontal cortex. The data or information you are inserting into your mind will tip the scale to one side of this battle.

1 John 2:15-16 NLT

Do not love this world nor the things it offers you, for when you love the world, you do not have the love of the Father in you. For the world offers only a craving for physical pleasure, a craving for everything we see, and pride in our achievements and possessions. These are not from the Father, but are from this world.

Another major sin problem is pride. As you might expect, the Bible associates pride with your eyes. C.S. Lewis hated pride as he says, "Pride leads to every other vice; it is the complete anti-God state of mind."

Isaiah 5:21 NLT

What sorrow for those who are wise in their own eyes
and think themselves so clever.

If you choose to sin, you will follow the limbic system's stimuli and desire or you will follow the Bible version of your brain and the flesh, by how you use your eyes. God wants you to turn from darkness and sin and look to Jesus, Who is the light of the world. Be very careful about what your eyes see. Matthew 6 says that the eye is like a lamp that provides light for your body. All that information makes changes to who you are. In 2 Corinthians 4:4, it says that Satan is busy at work, blinding people from understanding what they are seeing.

2 Corinthians 4:4 NLT

Satan, who is the god of this world, has blinded the minds
of those who don't believe. They are unable to see the
glorious light of the Good News. They don't understand
this message about the glory of Christ, who is the exact
likeness of God.

Two of my favorite verses in the Bible are Mathew 6:22-23 NLT.

Your eye is like a lamp that provides light for your body.
When your eye is healthy, your whole body is filled with
light. But when your eye is unhealthy, your whole body is
filled with darkness. And if the light you think you have is
actually darkness, how deep that darkness is!

There are several aspects to these Bible verses. If we look at this from a biological perspective, you have the ability to live a life of health and prosperity, if you have good vision. You have the opportunity to live a fruitful life in society. You have a better chance of having a good job and living a successful life. You can do those things without vision, but it will be a more challenging battle. Good vision can lead to a happier life.

What you look at determines how you feel. The more you look at things that negatively stimulate your limbic system, the unhealthier your body becomes. Stimulating your limbic system releases all kinds of chemicals and free radicals into the tissues of the brain and your body. The chemicals released from this stimulation lead to many diseases suffered by humanity. Therefore, what you spend your time watching, observing, and focusing on will eventually determine your body's health status.

These Bible verses say that your eyes have a direct relationship with your soul's health from a spiritual standpoint. As I said in the introduction, I believe that almost all sin begins or enters through your vision or eyes. If you spend your time looking at or observing good things, joyous things, honorable things, and righteous things, your soul will be full of the light of Jesus. Your spirit, mind, heart, and soul will be healthy. If you spend your time looking at pornography, violent acts, or other bad or negative things, your soul is going to be lost or dark.

The scary thing is in the last part of the verses, which says if you think you are doing great by observing these negative things, how deep is that darkness. You become blind to ultimate reality. Your perception of the world is altered or skewed like the Bible verse at the beginning of the chapter. You will be unaware of the darkness or your true circumstances. It may be a darkness you find yourself in that you cannot escape because your altered vision, perception, and reality keep you from seeing the truth. As the saying goes, "You don't know what you don't know." Even though your eyes see, your brain is not interpreting the signals from the eyes correctly. This unknown darkness is spiritually not a great place. It can become nearly impossible for you to perceive the reality of your circumstances.

There is a study in the *Journal Cognition* that studied the relationship between the eyes and the soul. Lead researcher Christina Starmans of the Mind and Development Lab at Yale and co-author Paul Bloom designed an experiment after a conversation one day. They discussed people's intuitive feelings as if one's consciousness or soul is located near the eyes. They tested 4-year-olds and adults. They showed them cartoon characters such as a green alien whose eyes were on its chest rather than its head. Both groups said that the character's consciousness or presence was located behind the eyes no matter where it was on the body. In other words, it appears that you learn to associate one's identity with the eyes. Your soul appears to be located behind your eyes!

Many people think that the statement "The eyes are the window to your soul" is in the Bible. Surprisingly, it was Willian Shakespeare who said it. The eye is a portal into your body, mind, soul, spirit, and heart.

Jesus commissioned Paul to open the eyes of the people.

Acts 26:17-18

Yes, I am sending you to the Gentiles to open their eyes, so they may turn from darkness to light and from the power of Satan to God.

In Luke 4:18, Jesus says that God sent him so that the blind will see. Paul says in Ephesians 1:18, I pray that the eyes of your heart (mind or soul) may be enlightened so that you may know the hope to which he has called you. Many people do not understand God's plan for their lives, not because they are not smart enough, but they lack perception, pure vision, or spiritual eyes. You may be able to read the bottom line on the chart in my office, but that does not mean your perception is correct. You may have 20/20 vision, but your perception has you blind as a bat, or your ability to perceive is like being in a coal mine at midnight!

Our basketball coach sent my teammates and me to the North Carolina State University basketball camp for two weeks one summer. The camp was in a big arena that contained four or five basketball courts. My friends and I were sitting in the stands during a break. We started talking about the rows of different colored seats in the stands across the arena. One of my friends, Milton, thought we were making it up or pulling a trick on him as he saw no seats. We could not convince him that there were rows of different colored seats on the other side of the arena. One of my other friends wears glasses as he was nearsighted. I asked Milton to put on Dusty's glasses. Milton screamed as he could see the seats with Dusty's eyeglasses on. Maybe that may be one reason Milton was not a great long-range shooter until he got his glasses! As soon as we returned home, he went to the eye doctor and got eyeglasses. I remember Milton telling me that he could not believe you could see the leaves on the trees after receiving his glasses. Until he put on Dusty's glasses, we could not convince him there were seats on the other side of the arena. Many people cannot understand or believe that their vision or perception is wrong. Because as far as you perceive or know it, everything you perceive or observe is perfect. Without spiritual eyes or pure vision, you will not have perfect perception or perceive ultimate reality. You may be nearsighted like Milton and have no idea that your vision is blurred, there are leaves on a tree, or multicolored seats are on the other side of the arena. Your perception of reality may be completely wrong.

David prays to God in Psalm 119:18 that he wants his eyes opened so that he will be able to see or know the truth in God's laws. Balaam delivered this message from God to Israel found in Numbers 24. Balaam says this is a message of the man whose eyes see clearly and the message of the one who hears the words of God. He who sees a vision from the Almighty and who bows down with eyes open. Balaam is telling Israel that he sees what the Spirit of God has shown him. He can see clearly because God's Spirit is giving him pure vision or spiritual vision. We need the Holy Spirit for us to have perfect perception or pure vision.

Here is maybe the best Biblical story about spiritual vision or pure vision. The king of Aram wanted to capture Elisha because God was using Elisha to give the King of Israel information on where the King of Aram would attack them. Elisha's information from God made it possible for Israel to keep thwarting the conquering army of King Aram from defeating Israel. The King of Aram learned where Elisha was staying and sent a large army with many chariots and horses to capture him. They surrounded the house where Elisha was staying during the night.

2 Kings 6:15-17 NLT

When the servant of the man of God got up early the next morning and went outside, there were troops, horses, and chariots everywhere. "Oh, sir, what will we do now?' the young man cried to Elisha. "Don't be afraid!" Elisha told him. "For there are more on our side than on theirs!" Then Elisha prayed, "O Lord open his eyes and let him see!" The Lord opened the young man's eyes, and when he looked up, he saw that the hillside around Elisha was filled with horses and chariots of fire.

Having spiritual vision or pure vision allows you to see what you were unable to see before. It would be amazing to have the ability to see into the spiritual world and to know what is going on behind what you can typically see. Everyone believes they are seeing perfectly and believes that what they see is true reality.

Through this book, I want to teach you how to see, really see. Helen Keller said, "The only thing worse than being blind is having sight but no vision." It is a shame that many people are oblivious to the world that surrounds them. People are easily led astray and blinded by Marxists believing people. As you will see in this book, you are being manipulated from all angles. What you choose to see and observe determines who you are as a person or who you will become. The secular world is after your soul. It is not only what your eyes are seeing that is important, but your perception of what your eyes are looking at is critical. When you choose to focus your eyes on good things or righteous things, you can understand that Jesus is the light of the world. Then you will know that Jesus is the way, the truth, and the life. You can develop or train yourself to have pure vision, spiritual vision, or try to see more as Jesus sees. Do not blind yourself from true or ultimate reality.

Blessed are they who see beautiful things in humble places where other people see nothing.

— Camille Pissarro

John 12:46 NLT

I have come as a light to shine in this dark world, so that all who put their trust in me will no longer remain in the dark.

Chapter 2

The Mystery and Miracle of Vision

Your mind composes what you see,
and you choose to see what you want to see.

— James E. Croley III, M.D.

Many people take their vision for granted. There is no effort required on your part for your eyes to see everything in your environment. Your vision miraculously occurs automatically. Your eyes focus on what you are looking at instantly without you telling your eyes anything. Vision is an incredible sense that God has given us. The intricacy, beauty, and symmetry of God's creation are stunning. God has given humankind and creatures the sight to function in the manner God designed for everything in the universe He created. Nearly everything you do in daily life involves sight or vision to perform. Without your eyes, you would not be in touch with your surroundings and the things happening around you. Without your eyes, you would never see colors or all the beautiful things in the world or truly understand what the word *beautiful* means. People born blind or who have lost their vision later in life can live a happy, fruitful life—but things are much more difficult for them.

Before you finish reading this sentence, nearly one hundred billion transactions have been performed in the eye. Unbelievable, right? You did not have to exert any effort for your vision to be miraculously present. The lens in your eye automatically focuses wherever you look. You do not have to calculate the eye muscles' precise actions, so your eyes can follow horses racing around a track. The brain automatically sends the proper signals to each of the six eye muscles to coordinate your eye movements. For this precision to occur, the muscle control for your eye's movement travels through many portions of your brain. The calculations and precision of your eye movements are phenomenal.

How did such a vitally important body function come into existence? How did a nonexistent concept of seeing suddenly appear in the world? Evolutionists claim that all living things in the world came into existence through a chain of total random coincidences, to develop the world as we know it. These claims defy all logic and common sense. Even though you never hear or read about it, many scientists have proven that all the evolution claims are unscientific, illogical, and based on forged evidence. This world cannot possibly be explained through coincidence and mutation. Science has shown that nearly one hundred percent of the time a mutation occurs, the process related to the mutation diminishes in function and does not improve function. There is no pathway to developing sophisticated organisms through mutations. It is just the opposite—nearly everything diminishes with each mutation. Evolution is impossible, as fossil evidence does not support the gradual development of creatures.

The eye and the miracle of vision have confused and puzzled evolutionists from the beginning. Darwin is quoted as saying, "I remember well the time when the thought that the eye made me cold all over." A close examination of the eye shows why evolutionists avoid talking about the evolution of the eye. The eye and vision are composed of many separate, distinct systems and components that only create vision when all are perfectly connected. If just one single system or structure is missing or not functioning, there is no vision. There is no possible pathway for the eye and vision to develop gradually through coincidence and mutation. There are just too many complexities, separate components, and no trial and error process through which evolution could result in the vision system.

When God said in the third verse in Genesis, "Let there be light," He could have added, "I will create my most prized creation with eyes that have the fantastic ability to use the light to see this beautiful world I have made."

The eye and the process of forming vision is a highly robust system. The human eye is composed of more than two million parts. Just think, you started as a single cell. This cell split into two cells, then into four. Millions and millions of further splits occurred until your body was completed. The cells contain DNA, which includes billions of bits of information and only the cells understand its directions. The DNA in cells keeps track of every portion of the body. A single cell develops into the human body according to the information in your DNA!

Under normal conditions, cell division would result in two identical cells. Therefore, you would expect millions of cells that are identical. During cell division, differences begin to occur. Cells differentiate themselves into the different parts of the body. How can two cells that are divided with the same DNA be so different from each other? Suddenly, at the right time of development, a cell starts to differentiate itself into cells for the eye. Science is unable to explain how cells decide to make such changes. How do the cells know when they need to develop eye cells? How do the cells find the correct genetic code for creating an eye from billions of DNA data points? How do the cells know which one will be a retinal cell and another cell will be an iris cell? It is a miracle and mystery that only God knows.

The theory of evolution cannot explain the development of the eye and vision. The eye and the portions of the brain responsible for vision are not directly connected. Therefore, they are useless by themselves. They would not slowly develop over millions of years since they are independent. No mutation or coincidence can account for the eye's complexity and intricacy and the brain's visual pathways. Mutations are like tornados—they typically destroy the structure and function wherever they occur.

Darwin's Theory of Evolution seems logical on the surface, but it does not conform to this theory when looking at the world God created. If humankind is the apex of evolution, we should have the best vision of all the creatures on earth. In the beginning, humankind would have depended on its eyesight for hunting for food. The person with the best vision would be the best hunter and survive, according to Darwin. Nearly fifty percent of people do not see 20/20 without glasses. How could a person survive on their hunting skills, if they could not see a rabbit twenty feet in front of them or a deer fifty feet away from them? If Darwin's theory is correct, only people with excellent vision would have survived in the past! (Note: Glasses were not invented until 1300 in Italy.)

Birds of prey such as eagles and hawks have a much deeper fovea in their retinas, giving them telephoto vision. These birds have seven to eight times better vision than humans. Tawny owls may have as high as one hundred times sharper vision. A cheetah can see an antelope three miles away. A chameleon's eyes rotate independently and can see monovision or binocularly. The tiny mantis shrimp has sixteen different cones in their retinas (compared to humankind's three cones) giving it the ability to have more profound and vivid colors. The Anableps fish has eyes adapted for seeing above and below the water with duplicated pupils, corneas, and photoreceptors in each eye. If you lived near water, this would have been a great advantage for hunting above the water and catching fish below the water.

If evolution existed, humankind (who is at the apex of development) should have the best vision. But that is not the case. There is no way people could have survived by hunting, if nearly half of them could not see without glasses. (Glasses were not invented until 1300.) It is time to put Darwin's Theory of Evolution on the shelf.

God created a perfect design when He created our eyes for the tasks before us. They are located in the best possible location. Situated on the head, you can turn your head to look to the side, which increases your viewing area without turning your body. Since more than half of your brain function is related to the eye and vision, they are located near the brain.

Six bone structures surround the eyes. The eyes are protected from harm by the brow, cheek, and nose. The eyes are separated by the right amount of distance to allow for depth perception. The eyes are bathed by the tear film, which contains the proper nutrients necessary to maintain a healthy eye surface. The muscles that move the eye are among the most active in the body. Over an average lifetime, the eye muscles move the eye billions of times.

Despite all this work, your eye muscles never seem to tire. The twelve eye muscles have to move in unison, so that you will not have double vision. The clear cornea in front of the eye is perfectly transparent, due to the delicate arrangement of fibers that comprise the cornea. There are no blood vessels in the cornea. So the cornea receives its nutrition from the tear film and oxygen from the air. Every cornea is shaped so that light is focused through the pupil onto the surface of the retina.

The fluid in the eye is produced by the ciliary processes and provides nutrients to the structures inside the eye. The iris is designed to protect the retina from too much exposure to light. The retina is composed of eleven microscopic layers of nervous tissue and is only 10 cm in area. The macula responsible for all your clear vision is 5 mm in diameter. The fovea, which is the exact center of your sharp vision, is only 1.5 mm in diameter. Amazingly, all of your fine reading ability is located in this tiny area! There are one hundred twenty million rod cells and six million cone cells in the retina. The retina changes its sensitivity to see under different light conditions. The retina can change its sensitivity by five hundred thousand to one million times!

The eye begins to develop during the first month of pregnancy. The eye is the second most complex system in the body, second only to the brain. Iris recognition is replacing fingerprints, as the iris has many more specific reference points. Fingerprints use 60 to 70 reference points compared to 200 to 250 reference points for the iris.

The optic nerve entering the eye is an extension of the brain. There are four lobes of the brain's cerebral cortex: the frontal lobe, temporal lobe, parietal lobe, and occipital lobe. The vision center for your eyes is located in the occipital lobe. Vision is complex and needs such a tremendous amount of brain function that the vision center requires one of the four lobes of your brain. Seven of the twelve cranial nerves are associated with the eye. Many different brain control areas control the eye movements required to stay focused on what you are watching. These eye movements are modulated by another section of the brain called the cerebellum.

Let us follow the pathway for your eyes to see. What is light that the eye can use to see? Light is an electromagnetic radiation, which is produced by vibrations of a charged material. There is a vast spectrum of electromagnetic radiation wavelengths, with visible light being only a small portion. Visible light waves have wavelengths between 400 and 700 nanometers. The colors of the rainbow are composed of these wavelengths.

The eye works in a very similar manner as a camera works. There is the front focusing lens of a camera. In the eye, the clear cornea and lens of the eye focus light into the eye. Light is focused onto the film of a camera or today onto a computer chip. Light is focused in the eye onto the retina. The retina has ten layers, but you may only remember the retina's rods and cones from school. These are the photoreceptors in the retina. As you may recall, the rods are for night vision and the cones are for color vision.

There is a unique part of the retina called the macula. The macula is a small area in the center of the retina. It is responsible for all of your fine, detailed, clear vision. This portion of the retina can degenerate as you age and is called macular degeneration. If you have macular degeneration, it is wise to take a supplement called the AREDS 2 formula to help maintain your macula's health.

Let us look at this miracle of vision and how it happens. The visual pathway starts as light enters the eye. The front surface of the eye, called the cornea, begins the focusing process for your vision. The light passes through the pupil and is then focused by the lens behind the pupil onto the retina. The light causes an electrochemical reaction in the rods and cones in the retina. This reaction is transmitted from the eye by the optic nerve out the back of the eye. The stimulus passes through the brain's entire structure to the occipital lobe in the back of the skull. In the brain, just behind the eyes, the optic nerves meet and separate to the right and left occipital lobes.

A remarkable thing happens at the optical nerves' meeting, half of the fibers from each eye crisscross. The vision stimulus from each eye divides. The right vision center in the brain sees the left half of your vision from each eye. The left vision center sees the right half of your vision from each eye.

Once the visual stimulus has reached the vision center, the brain has to form the vision and interpret what the eye sees. The vision center's two sides must communicate with each other and put each eye's vision back together. As the light passed through the pupil, it landed on the retina on the opposite side of the eye. So, your eye sees the opposite, which is upside down and reverse. The brain has to correct this orientation of your vision.

The visual stimulus reaches the primary visual cortex, primarily evaluating basic features of vision such as size, shape, edges, lines of orientation, topography, magnification, and movement. After the primary area has made changes to the visual stimulus, it transmits this information to the secondary visual cortex. The secondary visual cortex does more refining of the visual stimulus into more complex forms. The secondary visual cortex takes a stick figure as a child would draw to developing a three-dimensional, detailed, and colorful image.

The brain is still not finished with the visual stimulus. More information is needed to make a final determination of the image stimulus. The secondary visual cortex sends this image to two other brain portions: the temporal lobe and parietal lobe.

The parietal lobe processes the image information. This area of the brain provides information about the image's location in the environment or its spatial orientation. This orientation helps you function in your environment. You can locate the image, catch a ball, move your eyes to the image, or know exactly how to turn toward the visual image.

The temporal lobe plays a vital role in recognizing the character of the image. Phenomenally, research has shown that there may be specific neurons for each face that you know or have seen! The neuron will fire when it recognizes a match.

What about the colors you see? Your color vision is based on the trichromatic theory. The primary colors are blue, red, and green. Unbelievably, the eye can see up to ten million colors using three primary colors. Maybe you ladies might disagree with that, considering how many men choose their clothes! Many people have color vision problems, with eight percent of men and one-half percent of women having color vision loss. Eight percent of men do have an excuse!

Also, everything your brain decides about what you are seeing is based on context and prior experience. Context plays a significant role in what your brain decides about the image stimulus. You can fool your vision by context. Adjacent colors affect other surrounding colors. Because of this, you will have trouble seeing the correct color. The lighting source can also have a tremendous effect on colors or shades of color.

Another critical function of your vision is to be able to judge distance. Depth perception plays a vital role in many things that you do. You have to have good vision in both eyes to have depth perception. You need to see from two different directions for your brain to triangulate a distance.

The brain goes through a nearly endless number of visual stimulus evaluations, to arrive at what your brain determines the visual stimulus represents. The vision system is tremendously complex. Even your emotions can affect the way your brain sees. Your brain is continuously interpreting the images your eyes are sending. Here is a small number of the things the brain is evaluating about vision: space perception, relative size, position, familiar size, haze, aerial perspective, linear perspective, vanishing point, anamorphic projection, attention, visual search, feature search, guided search, and scene search.

As all of the different brain areas are assimilating this information about what you are observing, the brain needs to come to a conclusion. The vision information is sent to the prefrontal cortex in the frontal lobe to make a final decision. This decision leads to what is called *perception*. Your brain develops your vision in milliseconds continuously, as long as your eyes are open. On top of that, you really don't pay attention to all the things you are observing. The brain fills in the gaps of our insufficient attention with past experiences, which may or may not be correct. That is why people make many mistakes in perception.

Vision is a beautiful gift from God. The mystery of how just one single cell can convert light entering into the eye, into an electrochemical reaction useful for vision, is a miracle! One hundred twenty-six million retinal cells working in tandem, sending the electrochemical impulse from the eye through the entirety of the brain, to the vision center of the brain, is miraculous! There are 1.5 million nerve fibers in the small optic nerve exiting the eye on its way to the vision center. The nerves must match perfectly in the brain for there to be the vision you perceive. The vision center sends these impulses to many other portions of the brain to form your vision.

Vision is instant and is continuous, as long as your eyes are open. There are trillions of actions occurring to see an image for a split second. The mystery of vision remains a mystery. Science does not understand how all this is possible. Only a Designer, beyond our ability to understand, could perform the miracle of vision. People would be willing to give up a lot of things, instead of losing their sight.

God provided us with eyes and vision to live in His world. We are to use our eyes to live our lives in a Christian manner. What you spend time watching, molds and forms you into the person you will be or become. Warning, sin also enters your mind through your vision! God created the miracle of vision as a gift for us, in order to live in and perceive the beautiful world He created. God created vision to allow us to see Him in His creation.

As an ophthalmologist for over forty years, I am continually impressed by the miracle of vision. The mystery and miracle of vision is precious!

Psalm 104:24-25

O Lord, what a variety of things you have made! In wisdom you have made them all. The earth is full of your creatures. Here is the ocean, vast and wide, teeming with life of every kind, both large and small.

Vision is the art of seeing what is invisible to others.
Jonathan Swift

Our dreams are not limited by our abilities,
but by our ability to see.
— James E. Croley III, M.D.

Chapter 3
Paradigms or
Your Human Database

*Man's mind, once stretched by a new idea, never regains
its original dimensions.*

— Oliver Wendell Holmes

*One lives and analyzes data within a frame,
unaware that the solution is often just outside of that frame.
Never underestimate the depth of your subjectivity.*

— Darrell Calkins

The subject of paradigms became very popular in the 1980s
and 90s. You still hear about paradigms on occasions in the news
or other forms of information. You probably have an idea of what
comprises a paradigm, but you may not be aware of the extent to
which paradigms mold and shape your life. Paradigms make up
who you are as an individual, how you perceive this world, and
how you respond to what you believe is reality. Let us look at
some definitions of a paradigm.

Cambridge Dictionary *– Paradigm: A model of something, or
a very clear and typical example of something A set of theories that
explain the way a particular subject is understood at a particular
time*

Definition in *The Free Dictionary* – *One that serves a pattern or model; A set or list of all inflectional forms of a word or one of its grammatical categories; A set of assumptions, concepts, values, and practices that constitutes a way of viewing reality for the community that shares them, especially in an intellectual discipline.*

A paradigm is a set of assumptions, concepts, values, or practices that constitutes a way of viewing or receiving reality, accepted by a group or community as normal or scientifically correct.

Born in 1922 and died in 1996, Thomas Samuel Kuhn is one of the most influential philosophers of science of the twentieth century. His book, The Structure of Scientific Revolutions, published in 1962, is a sentinel book and one of the most cited books of all time. In his book, he stated that *paradigms are a global organizing model or theory with great explanatory power.* Kuhn was correct in saying, *Like all people, scientists see what they expect to see. Facts come clothed in history and colored by context.*

Paradigm comes from the Greek word "paradeigma" meaning *pattern, example, sample.* Thomas Kuhn used the theory of paradigms in a contemporary meaning, when he applied it to a set of concepts and practices that define a scientific discipline at any particular period of time. For well-integrated members of a specific discipline, its paradigm is so convincing that it renders even the possibility of alternatives unconvincing and counter-intuitive. A particular paradigm obscures the possibility that the paradigm might hide other alternative imageries. The conviction that the current paradigm is reality, tends to disqualify any evidence that might undermine the current paradigm. This rigid view of life results in paradigm paralysis or the inability or refusal to see beyond the current thinking models. A term with a similar meaning is *bias*.

Another way of describing a paradigm is that things or events are generally accepted as true or fact in the world, culture, religion, science, country, or political view. Changing a paradigm is very difficult or almost impossible in many instances. It may require a dramatic event or a new fact so powerful, it causes a new or different perception or paradigm. This change is called a *paradigm shift*. Many times, paradigm shifts face stiff opposition from the people tied to the old paradigm. You may be blinded by the power of your paradigm and are unable to see any new fact contrary to your paradigm or beliefs.

Joel Barker may be the most famous person who has written many books and lectured about paradigms. He used the concept of paradigms and paradigm shifts to explain how some companies succeed and others fail. Mr. Barker based a company's success on its willingness to think outside the box (paradigm) or explore new ways of doing things. Joel Barker talks about five components to strategic exploration and anticipation.

1. Influence understanding is to understand what influences your perceptions.

2. Divergent thinking means to develop thinking skills that could discover more than one answer.

3. Convergent thinking is using thinking skills to focus on integrated data and prioritize choices.

4. Mapping is important, in that we draw pathways to get from present to future.

5. Imaging processes picture words or drawings or models of the future as found in exploration.

These are important for companies, but they can also be applied to your personal life as well.

People and companies fall into what is called *habituation*. Habituation occurs when there is a decrease in response to a stimulus after repeated presentations. You stop paying attention to things in your environment. Enumerable processes are going on inside your brain that you rarely give full attention to, such as a particular event. You take things for granted. You follow the crowd or go with the flow. Companies tend to do the same thing. They are succeeding in the way they currently do things and become complacent. Many companies have gone bankrupt. They failed to see outside of their paradigm and could not see the changes coming their way. They were blinded by their inability to see anything other than their current paradigm.

Xerox failed to shift its paradigm and pursue laser printers, graphical interfaces, and Ethernet.

Kodak had 170,000 employees in 1998. At one point, Kodak sold 85% of all the photo paper in the world. Kodak went bankrupt, because they ignored the digital revolution. Digital cameras were invented in 1975, but they had a very low resolution. Kodak did not see them as a threat. The digital camera began to advance and developed high-resolution chips. Kodak was finished!

Another famous story about a failure to look outside of their paradigm is about the Seiko quartz watch. The Swiss are renowned for making fine intricate mechanical watches. The Swiss craftsmanship was unsurpassed. Swiss engineer Max Hetzel developed an electric wristwatch with non-moving parts. The quartz watch is much simpler, more reliable, and more accurate. Because the Swiss thought all watches needed to be hand-made with fine intricate moving parts, they never would produce a quartz watch. In 1974, the Swiss produced nearly 45 million watches a year.

A Japanese company called Seiko brought the first analog quartz watch to the market in 1969, called the Seiko Quartz Astron. The Swiss paradigm never allowed themselves to see the shift occurring in watches, even though a Swiss watchmaker developed the quartz watch. By 1983, the number of Swiss watch exports fell to approximately 3 million. That is 45 million to only 3 million watches!

In 1978, Polaroid employed 21,000 people. Polaroid's instant cameras were a huge success. Everyone was taking pictures with these cameras. The film would pop out of the camera and the image would develop right before your eyes. You had a picture in 60 seconds! In 1978, there were 14 million Polaroid cameras sold in the United States. But Polaroid did not see the coming of digital cameras and went bankrupt in 2001.

The evolution of Sears is what America is all about. Sears was a retail staple since the Civil War. At the end of the 19th century, Sears was an early innovator when it launched its mail-order catalog. If you are old enough, you will remember getting it in the mail and fervently looking to see what was in the new catalog. Sears was the largest retailer in the world.

In 1969, Sears employed 355,000 people. It began construction on the world's tallest skyscraper, the Sears Tower. How is it possible that the retailor of the premier brands in America (such as Kenmore appliances, Craftsman tools, the Discover credit card, and the World-War era Sears homes, which helped thousands of families realize their dream of homeownership) failed? Like many other companies, they were unable to see the changing business environment. Sears' downfall was self-inflicted! Its failure to change its thinking doomed it to failure. Companies like Walmart began to take away their market share. Sears ultimately lost the game, because of its reluctance to believe in the reality of a rapidly changing retail marketplace. Their paradigm froze them in place.

Before Apple's iPhone arrived on the scene, Blackberry was the first choice in mobile phones. By 2007, the company made 3 billion dollars with a net of 631 million. Blackberry sold 50 million phones in 2011. Blackberry controlled 50 percent of the smartphone business in the United States and 20 percent worldwide. In 2006, Apple and Google had no relationship with the carriers. The Blackberry phone had a simple design, was easy to use, and had a full keyboard on the phone.

Blackberry had all the government contracts. I remember going into the Senate and Congressional offices in Washington, D.C. You could only take a Blackberry into the offices. All other phones were barred as they had a camera. The Blackberry did not have a camera. They did not want you to take pictures in the Congressional and Senate offices. (Of course, that has changed now.) Blackberry stayed focused on its current customers selling a few million phones and missed out on the billions to come. It failed to change its phone platform to meet market demands. In 2016, a Chinese consumer-electronic company bought the Blackberry phone, which led to its removal from the smartphone market.

The fall of Blockbuster is another example of a closed paradigm culture in a company. Blockbuster was founded by David Cook and opened its first store in Dallas, Texas on October 19, 1985. Blockbuster developed an innovative barcode system that could track up to 10,000 VHS tapes per store to each registered customer—which meant they could easily track late fees. Remember those late fees? In one year, they made 800 million in late fees alone. In the late 1990s, Blockbuster owned over 9,000 video rental stores in the United States. They employed 84,000 people and had 65 million registered customers. Cook sold Blockbuster to Huizenga. Huizenga sold Blockbuster to media giant Viacom for 8 billion dollars in 1994.

While John Antioco of Viacom focused on its brick-and-mortar video stores, other companies innovated new technologies. Reed Hastings founded Netflix in 1997, in part because he was upset with a $40 late fee from Blockbuster. Netflix offered a DVD-by-mail service with no late fees. Around 2007, Netflix transitioned from DVD by mail to online streaming. At one point, Netflix approached Blockbuster about buying them out for 50 million dollars. They offered to run the Blockbuster brand online for them. Blockbuster refused. Their paradigm was stuck on their brick-and-mortar stores. Blockbuster was so in love with their business model, they could not see the future of the video and movie business. They honestly thought that their brick-and-mortar stores would forever be the most preferred method.

In 2010, Blockbuster filed for bankruptcy with nearly 1 billion dollars of debt. A $40 late fee inspired someone to develop a new paradigm in the video rental business—and Blockbuster never saw it, even though it was right in front of them. It is hard to believe that something as simple as a late fee inspired the development of a gigantic online company. But that is how paradigms work. Many people and companies are wearing blinders and cannot see.

How are paradigms formed in your brain? How do paradigms work in your personal everyday life? Your brain is a highly complex organ that does not completely mature until you are in your mid-twenties. There are four major components of the central nervous system: the spinal cord, brainstem, midbrain or limbic system, and the cerebral hemispheres.

- The spinal cord carries messages to and from the brain throughout the body.
- The brainstem is responsible for routine body functions, such as breathing, heart rate, and other essential body functions.
- The limbic system is responsible for your emotions, such as fear, worry, stress, sex drive, and rage, for a few.
- The limbic system is the center of your fight or flight response.

The cerebral hemispheres are what distinguishes humankind from other animals. The cerebral hemispheres are the part of the brain responsible for thinking, contemplating, and making rational decisions. In people, the emotional limbic system is constantly battling with the logical decision-making cerebral hemispheres. Which portion of the brain dominates a person results in the type of person they become.

Until recently, scientists felt that your brain was rigid. After you mature, most scientists believed your brain could not form new brain cells or neural pathways—the brain could not change once you were an adult. The old saying that *you cannot teach an old dog new tricks* is not correct. The brain has significant plasticity or the ability to grow or change. Your brain is in a constant state of flux. Every single second new neurons are being formed and new circuits of axons are being developed. Also, neurons that go unused over time are trimmed or pruned away. Your beliefs or paradigms have the ability to change over time. You do not think the same way you did when you were younger.

In many respects, your brain is like a computer filled with large volumes of information or data. The brain is about the size of a cantaloupe and weighs about three pounds. It is composed of eighty percent water and sixty percent of the tissue is composed of lipid or fat. There may be more than one thousand miles of blood vessels in the brain. The brain has tremendous storage capacity and contains about five times the information found in a set of encyclopedias. There are one hundred billion neurons or brain cells in the brain, with one quadrillion connections or synapses. You could fit thirty thousand neurons on the head of a pin! There are over one hundred thousand miles of myelinated axons in the brain. The brain can perform as many as one hundred trillion calculations per second! Yes, I said one hundred trillion calculations per second. Your brain is constantly processing enormous volumes of data or information. You are consciously aware of only a tiny portion of the data processing at any one moment.

Approximately seventy percent of brain function is processing information from your five senses. Eighty-three percent of that is related to vision. More than fifty percent of the brain's cortex is processing visual information. Vision is a staggeringly complex process that involves a tremendous amount of brain function. Most of the data information going into your brain is received from your eyes. That is why what you choose to observe is so critical. You are continually putting new data into your brain that it will use in the future.

You cannot unsee what you have seen! If you take the time to think about this seriously, it can be a very frightening realization. You cannot erase, remove, or expunge images from your mind or brain that you have seen. You can try to suppress or forget them, but your vision memories will remain in the repository vision center forever. This permanent memory bank is especially true for images that are connected to a significant emotional event. These images or experiences will add or change your paradigm. If you have some traumatic or exhilarating event in your life, it is almost impossible to keep those images out of your consciousness. You hear people say, "I cannot get that image out of my mind." Your eyes are the gateway to the image storage center of your mind. Every day you are adding an almost inexhaustible number of new images or experiences. They are in your mind, no matter what you think about them. These images may be joyful, sad, harmful, or useless—and you cannot discard them. What you choose to have your eyes look at is permanent for the rest of your life. If you carelessly look at things or decide to look at harmful things, those images are stored in your mind for life. As I said before, you cannot unsee what you have seen. All these images, data, and experiences are deposited in your mind. All of this data comprises the details of your paradigm.

You choose what to look at and spend time watching. You are aware of only a tiny portion of the things you are observing. Obviously, many things that you see in daily life cannot be avoided. But you do have the choice of what you spend time consciously focusing on, studying, or watching. You have custody of your eyes.

Let us examine paradigms and how they work in your personal life. Everything that you study, observe, read, research, listen to, watch on television, see on a computer, look at a smartphone, events in the world, and the instances that happen to you in your life mold or form your paradigm. Most of the time, you control those things, but some circumstances can occur beyond your control. Tragic events such as losing a loved one, traffic accident, illness, and other significant emotional events play a vital role in your paradigm. Your paradigm is unique to you. All these experiences of your life are unique to you. Twins will be different, because they will not have the same experiences. They may be similar in many ways, but will have a different paradigm.

What is the relationship between what we see and how we perceive? What about the interaction of observation and perception related to past experiences and expectations? Paradigms comprise the world-views of individuals, companies, countries, religions, cultures, societies, regions of nations, and cities. The people living in the southern United States have their cultures or paradigms. The people on the West Coast have different beliefs than people in the Midwest. The people around you continually influence the characteristics of your personality. Your brain will be conditioned to think in a specific way by your environment. The world view you live in is continuously reinforcing your current paradigm.

For centuries, people believed that the world was flat. Even though a Greek astronomer named Eratothenes mathematically proved that the Earth was round in 300 B.C. He calculated the curvature and size of the Earth within two percent! Very few people believed him, as they thought it was impossible for the Earth to be round. How would people not fall off a round world? What would keep everyone attached to the ground? They were locked in their paradigm of the world being flat. It was not until Magellan's group circled the globe in 1522 that people believed the world was round.

You can have a tremendous effect on someone, just by what you say to them. You can change someone's thought process or paradigm. There was a study by a company that specializes in paradigms and how they affect the world. They went to an NFL team during preseason workouts. They interviewed half of the players and told them how fantastic they looked. They complimented them and asked them what they were doing to look so strong and healthy. They measured and recorded their chest size, arms, and legs. Then, they told the other half of the players that they did not look well. They looked weak and tired. They asked them if they were handling the preseason workouts well. They measured their chest size, arms, and legs.

Two weeks later, they went back and did the same thing, but this time they reversed what they told each group. They said to the group that was doing great and looked strong that they were not looking so well. The group not doing well was now doing fantastic. They remeasured them and looked at the differences. The chest measurements between being told how great they looked versus how weak they looked was 1 ½ inches—just being told how great or bad they looked changed them physically. Paradigms have powerful influences on your life. They affect how you feel, your health, everything you do, and how you react to everything in your life.

There is an excellent story about paradigms where blind men examine an elephant. Six men were born blind in a village. All the people in the village watched over them, to protect them from harm or danger. The men heard stories about elephants and became curious. What was an elephant really like? The villagers told them stories about how large they were, how powerful they were, and how loud their trumpet calls were. The men would argue back and forth about elephants. One would say they are powerful giants. The next man would say they are kind and gentle giants, since princesses ride on their backs. The next man would argue that the elephant is very dangerous, as it can pierce through a man with a sharp horn. The next man says all of them are wrong—they are just big cows. And one of the men said that elephants do not even exist.

Finally, the villagers got tired of their arguing and made arrangements for the blind men to meet an elephant. The first blind man touched the elephant's side. He said that it was huge and smooth like a wall and that it must be very powerful. The second blind man touched the elephant's trunk and said it was like a giant snake. The third blind man touched the hard-pointed tusk and said that the elephant is sharp and deadly as a spear. The fourth blind man touched one of the elephant's legs and said it was a large cow. The fifth blind man touched one of the elephant's ears and said it was like a giant fan or magic carpet that could fly. The sixth man touched the elephant's tail and said it is just like a piece of rope.

So the blind men are still arguing over what an elephant is, as each had a different experience or perception.

The story about the blind men is an excellent example of how a paradigm works. You have your own set of experiences, which ultimately determines how you evaluate everything in your life. You can see how paradigms alter your perception. Your present paradigm determines what you perceive and understand. It also results in what your reaction is to a particular circumstance. Just like in the elephant story, your paradigm may lead you to a very wrong or lousy conclusion. Let us look at some picture examples to see how paradigms work.

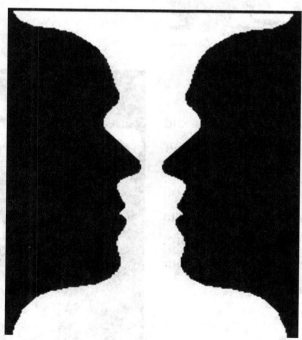

What do you see? Did you see a vase or two people facing each other, or did you see both images quickly? Your paradigm will direct you to what you see or which way you see it when you first look at it.

Did you see the face looking to the left, or did you see an Eskimo facing to the right?

Do you see a face, or did you see the word liar? Your paradigm will determine how you process the visual input. You will see what your brain's data produces. What you interpret or perceive is based on your particular paradigm.

Do you remember this type of image? The image above is a Rorschach test image. The Rorschach Test is a psychological test developed by Hermann Rorschach in 1921. The design of the test measures any thought disorder for diseases like schizophrenia. The person is shown ten inkblot images and asked to identify what they see in the inkblot. Some psychologists use this test to examine a person's personality and emotional status or function. The underlying assumption is that you will classify external visual stimuli based on personal-specific perceptual sets, prior experience, knowledge, or stored data and process this into real-life situations. The Rorschach Test can be thought of as a psychometric examination of pareidolia. The mind's paradigm allows you to observe or see things in your environment. What you see is the result of how your mind processes information, based on the storage of data present in the brain. Pareidolia is the tendency for the incorrect perception of an object, pattern, or meaning known to the observer in your vision. Examples are seeing shapes in clouds, faces in inanimate objects, or seeing objects in abstract patterns. A famous example is the man in the Moon. You can see a face with just a few lines.

Pareidolia was considered to be a form of human psychosis many years ago. Vision and perception have been used as a method of diagnosing mental disease. Those types of theories have diminished over time. But it is true that the way your mind perceives the images your eye is observing, corresponds directly to how your mind processes data and information.

Pareidolia is used in computer programs and for artificial intelligence. Software programs are given large numbers of examples of medical abnormalities and use that data to find a new disease. Computer software programs examine X-Rays, MRIs, and C.T. scans. Artificial intelligence scans for eye diseases on OCT scans of the retina based on pareidolia.

Mimetoliths are rock formations that mimic known forms through random formations, weathering, and erosion. One famous rock formation is in Jerusalem. Calvary is the name by which we know the Biblical site of Golgotha, meaning *place of the skull,* where they crucified Jesus. This site outside of the north wall of Jerusalem's old city on Mount Moriah is identified as one of the possible locations of Jesus' crucifixion.

We do not know if this formation looked the same 2,000 years ago, but it is intriguing to contemplate, if you get the opportunity to visit this place.

Graphic artists often use pareidolia in paintings and drawings. There are religious instances of pareidolia. Most of them are images of Jesus and the Virgin Mary. There was a famous instance of the face of the Virgin Mary in a grilled cheese sandwich. In the 1980s, there was an instance of seeing Jesus in the sky of Eastern Europe for a few months. A nurse from my hospital went and stared into the sky, looking for Jesus for a whole day. The sun burned her macula in both eyes and she lost a portion of her vision from the sun damage. You should never stare at the sun, as the intensity of the light coming from the sun can permanently damage your retina.

Your brain is hardwired to evaluate all the images your brain receives. All of your previous images and experiences are stored in the brain like a computer. You have a personal database that is always expanding and storing new information. Everything of significance you look at is stored. You cannot hit the delete button.

That is why you should control where and what your eyes observe. Past images will have an influence on the manner in which you process all the new sensory information around you. You live your existence by all the sensory input your brain is processing.

Humankind lives its life by examining the relationship between what it sees and what it determines is real. Man learns about the interaction of observation and perception in the presence of experience and expectation. Paradigms determine how you perceive and store the input from your senses, especially your vision.

Paradigms are vital in the understanding of your environment or life experiences. There is so much sensory information bombarding your mind. It is impossible to be aware of everything all the time. Your mind tends to jump around and not stay entirely focused. You tend to develop habits, get in ruts, and many times things are on autopilot. During these gaps of attention, your mind fills in these gaps from your paradigm or past experiences. In many instances, it may not be correct. You are not under any circumstances always aware of everything that your senses are sending to your brain.

Often we don't realize that our attitude toward
something has been influenced by the number of times
we have been exposed to it in the past.

— Robert B. Cialdini

Try this experiment for a couple of minutes. Try and focus for one minute on all the sensory input in the place where you are sitting. Listen to all the sounds in the room. Maybe you hear the air-conditioning turning on, the hum of an appliance, the sound of a clock ticking, and any other sounds around you. How comfortable is the chair or couch where you are sitting? Is one particular spot not as comfortable as another place? Scan around the room and look at all the different colors, shades of colors, textures, shapes, and sizes. What about any smells or scents in the room? Do you sense any other sensations in your body that you were aware of before? How about the temperature in the room and any tastes in your mouth? You will not be able to monitor all these sensations at one time. Trying to do this for just a minute is tiring.

Now, go back to your routine daily activities. Are you still paying attention to all those things you sensed before? It is impossible! Your senses are continually sending information to your brain. It is still processing all that information in your surrounding environment. All but a finite amount of sensory data goes to your subconscious mind. Your nose is still smelling everything, but you will not be aware of it unless you smell something different or unusual. There is so much information being processed that your mind sends most of the data to your subconscious. Your mind chooses what it wants to be conscious of seeing.

Paradigms color your perception by filtering and prioritizing information and fills in the gaps of your awareness with what your paradigm thinks is relevant. Your state of mind can dramatically alter your paradigm processing. During an emotional event, your ability to correctly process all the sensory information will be severely hindered.

Eyewitnesses to crimes are incorrect many times. The stimulation of their limbic system and emotions alters their perceptions. Their paradigm related to the crime observed will skew their perception. You tend to have altered perceptions and make poor decisions during stressful times.

Paradigms determine how you live your life and react to the circumstances in your life. The data instilled into your brain makes up your paradigm. You have heard the saying in the computer world—*garbage in garbage out*. Fill in your human database with Christian thoughts or information and good things. Your paradigm does not like change. It keeps you from seeing things outside of your paradigm. You are unaware of truths that may be in front of you. Paradigms, as you have learned, can blind a company or an individual. Paradigms usually change very minimally or slowly, but a significant emotional event can change your paradigm almost instantly. As I said in my first book, Believing Is Seeing, you need to focus through a God-centered paradigm. A Christian paradigm is essential. God needs to be where your mind is grounded. Make sure that you are open to the reality before you. Pure vision, focused through a stable Christian paradigm, leads to perfect perception, which is discussed in the next portion of the book.

1 Corinthians 13:12 NLT

Now we see things imperfectly, like puzzling reflections in a mirror, but then we will see everything with perfect clarity.

1 Corinthians 13:12 MSG

We don't yet see things clearly. We're squinting in a fog, peering through a mist. But it won't be long before the weather clears and the sun shines bright!

Everyone needs to be molding and changing their paradigms in a positive Christian manner. You need to put fabulous experiences into your paradigm!

Chapter 4

Perfect Perception

The eye sees only what the mind is prepared to comprehend.

— Robertson Davies

One has not only an ability to perceive the world, but an ability to alter one's perception of it; more simply, one can change things by the manner in which one looks at them.

— Tom Robbins

Jesus is the only man with perfect perception. Humankind will never have or be able to develop perfect perception, but everyone should strive to obtain the closest to perfect perception as possible. Excellent perception is essential for living a rich and full life. Excellent or perfect perception is one of the most essential functions your eyes and mind perform. Striving toward perfect perception requires you to have faith in God, as God created the world where we live. Perfect perception requires a Christian paradigm to guide your perception. A God-centered paradigm is the most crucial step in your journey in striving towards perfect perception. The Bible is your playbook for living your life.

The Reformed theologian, John Calvin, compares Scripture to a pair of spectacles that enables you to see the world in the proper context. The Bible is like eyeglasses that allow you to see God. Calvin says in his published <u>Institutes of the Christian Religion,</u>

> *For as the aged, or those whose sight is defective, when any book, however fair, is set forth before them, though they perceive that there is something written, are scarcely able to make out two consecutive words, but, when aided by glasses, begin to read distinctly, so Scripture, gathering together the impressions of Deity, which, till then, lay confused in our minds, dissipates the darkness, and shows us the true God clearly.*

> *For just as eyes, when dimmed with age or weakness or by some other defect, unless aided by spectacles, discern nothing distinctly; so, such is our feebleness, unless Scripture guides us in seeking God, we are immediately confused.*

So, Scripture needs to be your guide to perfect perception. In this chapter, I will present to you many other factors which will contribute to your perception. Let us first begin with some definitions of perception.

Google:

- *The ability to see, hear or become aware of something through the senses*

- *The state of being or the process of becoming aware of something through the senses*

- *A way of regarding, understanding, or interpreting something; a mental impression*

- *Intuitive understanding and insight*

Cambridge Dictionary:

- *A belief or opinion, often held by many people and based on how things seem*

- *The quality of being aware of things through physical senses, especially sight*

- *Someone's ability to notice and understand things that are not obvious to other people*

- *A thought, belief, opinion, often held by many people and based on appearances*

- *The way that someone thinks and feels about a company, product, service, etc.*

- *Synonyms for perception are awareness, consciousness, recognition, conception, discernment, observation, apprehending, and realizing.*

Perception is demonstrably an active process rather than a passive process; it constructs rather than records 'reality'.

— Michael Michalko

Some people categorize perception into internal, external, or a mix of internal and external perception. Internal perception is concerned with what is going on inside your body, such as feeling tired, hungry, standing, sitting, hot, or cold. External perception is affected by what is happening in the world around your body. Mixed perception tells you what is going on in your body and the perceived outward cause of perceptions acting on your body.

Your paradigm and the context of what you observe are two of the significant components of determining your perception. What do I mean by perfect perception, and why is it important? Jesus had perfect perception. As I said, everyone should strive to have the most accurate perception possible. Great perception leads to a better life, making better decisions, and living a life closer to God.

You are very knowledgeable concerning paradigms and how they work now. Another significant effect on perception is context. So, let us look to see how context affects your perception.

Let us compare what you can see from a mountain top perspective to a valley perspective. Throughout humankind's history, mountain tops have engendered a sense of awe, majesty, challenge, a place of power, and mystery. It is the location of mystical gods, according to the Greek and Roman religion before Christianity. A mountain top experience is mentioned in the Bible hundreds of times and is the location of many special events. Mount Sinai, Mount Tabor, Mount of Olives, Calvary, and the Sermon on the Mount, are just a few. Abraham offered his son Isaac on Mount Moriah. Mount Ararat is where Noah's ark landed. Mount Sinai is where God revealed Himself to Moses and gave him the Ten Commandments. There are many recordings of mountain top experiences with Jesus.

The greatest teaching sermon ever occurs on the Mount, where Jesus gave the Beatitudes. Jesus' last teaching before being arrested and crucified happened on the Mount of Olives, where He explained the world's future. There is the Mount of Transfiguration, where Jesus revealed Himself in His glory talking with Moses and Elijah. Jesus took His three closest disciples to the mountain top to reveal His majesty to them. Mountain tops are where heaven and earth are the most intimate.

Mountain top experiences can take your breath away. The view of the world from the top of a mountain provides an entirely different perspective or context, than the view of life in the valley. You sometimes need a panoramic view to see God's plan for your life. You do not want to be mired down in the valley with no hope of seeing out in the distance. You do not want to live life without a vision of your destiny. Instead, you want to have the hope of Jesus Christ as your guide into the future. Sometimes hope is difficult to see while in the valley.

Mountain top views give you a panorama of the world that you cannot see from the valley. You are elevated way above your usual way of seeing, while in the valley. From the mountain top, you can see out in the distance different parts of the world. Lookout Mountain in Chattanooga, Tennessee is famous for seeing seven states—assuming you are good at geography and know which state is in which direction. Things from a mountain top seem tiny in the valley. Depending on the height of the mountain, a car may even be difficult to see. From a spiritual or life standpoint, the valley's troubles are tiny specs of little significance from the mountain top or from a Christian view or according to God's perspective. Once you are a Christian, you have already started your eternal life with God. Things that happen here on Earth are a tiny speck in relation to your life in eternity! The mountain top view helps you keep your focus out in the distance. Heaven and God is your ultimate destination.

Everything is up close in the valley, right in front of you, and you have limited visibility. You may have trouble seeing beyond your current situation. Since I am an ophthalmologist, let us look at this from an eyesight perspective. When you are in the valley, you have myopia or are nearsighted. You are unable to see out in the distance. You can only see what right is in front of you.

Everything in the distance is out of focus. When you are on the mountain top, you have hyperopia or are farsighted. You have clear distance vision. You can see far out in the distance. Everything up close does not seem as important. You can see the path to your destination out in the distance.

The valley of life is changing rapidly today. Many years ago in the United States, nearly everyone believed in God. The valley of today makes it difficult or almost impossible to believe there is a God! The human perception of today is almost unrecognizable from just a few years ago. Humanity is too intelligent and educated to believe in an unseen God.

Romans 1:20 NLT

For ever since the world was created, people have seen the earth and sky. Through everything God made, they can clearly see his invisible qualities—his eternal power and divine nature. So they have no excuse for not knowing God.

If you take the time to observe the awe-inspiring intricate design in the universe, you conclude that there is a divine designer. But, everyone thinks they are in control of their destiny. The valley is full of muck, treachery, deceit, and temptations, which many people fail to see. Pride gets in the way and skews your perception. A mountain top view allows you to awaken to a reality that you cannot see in the valley. Though there are times that it takes the valley to knock you down, to stimulate you to climb the mountain. Sometimes it takes a significant emotional event or deep or low experience to awaken the desire or need that the valley or the secular world cannot satisfy. Deep valleys help people to search for God and can be the motivation to change. When things seem broken, helpless, troubled, dark, and there is no hope, you realize you may need a different way. The Puritans called this paradoxical experience *the valley of vision*. Often, the valley view causes you to look up toward the top of the mountain where you can find God. There the mountain's view confirms what the valley's view was trying to show you. Once you are a Christian, you are a new person. Now with the guidance of the Holy Spirit, your perception begins to change.

After experiencing *the valley of vision*, you should be able to walk up to the mountain top and look at life from this new perspective. Many people who write about this subject believe you always live in the valley with its limited view or perspective. The view from the mountain top is a rare occasion. In the valley of everyday life, you live your life with limited perspective and possibly diminished hope. Once you are a Christian, the valley view is different because you have been to the mountain top. You have started your journey of eternal life. You have seen your new destiny out on the horizon from your mountain top perspective. Your new Christian view is forever.

Living on the side of a mountain in a small town in Eastern Appalachia, I always had a mountain view that looked down over my small town. I grew up with a mountain view every day. I loved growing up with that view. Now, there were times when I was walking home up the mountain that I might have wished that I lived down in the valley! But the benefit was that I developed strong legs, which were great for sports. As a Christian, your faith and closeness to God improves or strengthens with the journeys up the mountain. The air and environment on top of the mountain are cleaner. Other Christians are there enjoying the mountain top view, with whom you can develop relationships. Your faith develops strong legs climbing the mountains of life!

I think that the mountain top view I had every day helped me look at life from a unique perspective. I have always looked at the big picture. When things got tough, I was able to keep my focus on the distance. During my medical training, there were many long grueling hours of study and work. I could have easily gotten stressed with the feeling that the day was never going to end, or there was no light at the end of the tunnel. What kind of emergency is going to come through the door to the hospital? When you are down in the valley of turmoil, you need to have the mountain top view in your mind.

One of the most powerful factors in perception is context. Context has a tremendous effect on the colors you see. Context dramatically alters your perception of colors. A surrounding color will change your perception of an adjacent color. You can test this yourself by buying colored paper. Cut a hole in the colored paper and place it over a different color and observe the difference. Neighboring colors change the appearance of other colors. Artists are very aware of how context affects the colors of their paintings.

Lukewarm water may feel cold or hot, depending on context. If you hold your hand in ice water for a couple of minutes and put your hand in lukewarm water, it will feel like hot water. If you heat your hand in a heating pad for several minutes, the lukewarm water will feel cool or cold. You need to understand the impact context has on your perception of life to develop perfect perception.

Here is another way context can influence your perception. Psychologist Dennis Proffitt of the University of Virginia performed an experiment or study on perception. They had people stand on either a skateboard or a box of the same height as the skateboard on top of a hill. They were instructed to look down the slope and judge its grade or steepness. During the test, they asked the participants how afraid they felt about descending the hill. The fearful people on the skateboards judged the hill to be steeper than the unafraid people standing on the boxes. This study leads to another thing influencing your perception. Fear or other emotional states change your perception.

In golf, when you feel like you are putting well, the hole looks bigger. When you are in a putting slump, the hole appears tiny and the ball never goes in. It is the same for many other sports. A baseball looks big when you are hitting well—and the basketball goal is enormous when you are making every shot.

As you can see, context and emotions play a tremendous role in your ability to perceive and correctly understand this world. What other things do we know about perception?

Perception results from signals from the five senses and is carried to the brain by an electrochemical process. The perceptual system of the brain enables you to see the world as stable, even though the sensory input is usually incomplete and rapidly changing. As discussed with paradigms, you fill in the missing data from past experiences. Another significant factor influencing perception is motivation. It is like the old saying, "Is the glass half full or half empty." Your emotional state or outlook on life will alter your perceptions. Your mental state affects your readiness or preparedness of your mind's ability to process the sensory information the brain is receiving. Your motives, desires, or needs will significantly influence your perception. Therefore, you do not see things as they appear, but you see them as you want to see them.

> *No two people see the external world in exactly the same way. To every separate person a thing is what he thinks it is-- in other words not a thing but a think.*
>
> — Penelope Fitzgerald

Errors in perception may be due to knowledge or your paradigm being inappropriate or misapplied. In many cases, your hidden censor or paradigm will not let you see things as they are. Many studies on perception show that you have trouble seeing anything that you are not focused on or is outside of your attention. I showed a short video to one hundred men during a lecture on paradigms. In the video, there were two groups of three girls walking back and forth between each other. The three girls in white shirts were passing a ball back and forth to each other. The three girls in black shirts were also passing a ball back and forth to each other. I challenged the men to count how many times the girls in the white shirts passed the ball to each other.

Thirty seconds into the video, one of the girls in a black shirt near the edge of the screen left the group. Simultaneously, a person in a gorilla costume entered the group. In the middle of the screen, the gorilla stopped and beat its chest. Then slowly everyone left the scene. I asked how many times the girls in the white shirts passed the ball. They proudly replied sixteen times. They were making sure they got the number correct. I asked how many men saw the gorilla. Astonishingly, only ten of the men saw the gorilla in the scene. The gorilla had stopped right in the middle of the scene and pounded on its chest! How could anyone not see this colossal gorilla? The men thought I was making it up! When I replayed the video, they accused me of playing a different video! Their attention was occupied with one thing, counting the number of passes by the girls in the white shirts. Their attention on the girls caused them to fail to notice something right before their very eyes.

When you learn about these studies, they may seem unreal and strange. How is it possible that you continuously fail to notice things right in front of you? Is there some mysterious force keeping you from seeing something right there? In fact, people continually overlook or fail to see much of the world right in front of them. When you focus your mind on one thing, you miss other things in your environment that might be extremely important. Your paradigm or censor will screen them out or fill in gaps from your human database.

Your mind calculates trillions of pieces of information a second. You can only be aware of a finite amount. The simple fact of selectivity has vast consequences! Your unconscious mind contains a massive amount of information, biases, and stereotypes unique to you. Your mind is limited in the information it can handle at any single moment. Selectivity means that your unconscious mind or paradigm shapes your experience. Your mind is programmed to be aware of dangerous things quickly and will break your attention as a means of preservation. Those things will be brought to your consciousness immediately. But, the unconscious mind and the associated paradigm shapes what your conscious mind gets to see. The unconscious mind has a head start.

Many times, things may appear as illusions. An illusion is a thing that is likely to be wrongly perceived or interpreted by your senses. An illusion may occur naturally in the world or may be an act of deception. Magicians use illusions to fool you or make you think it is magic. There are all kinds of illusion illustrations that are interesting to view and ponder.

There are two types of illusions—those with a physical cause and cognitive illusions due to the misapplication of knowledge. Physical illusions may be due to disturbances of light between objects and the eyes. Cognitive illusions are due to misapplied knowledge by the brain, interpreting sensory information. The Muller-Lyer illusion is an excellent example of an illusion. The middle straight lines are the same length.

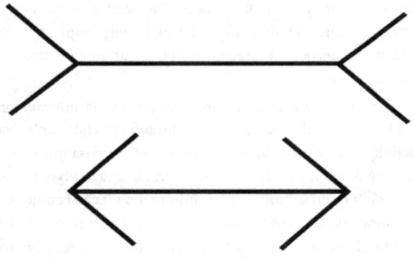

What other things alter your perception? First impressions can significantly affect your perception. First impressions can have a lasting impact on your perception of something or someone and it may be hard to change. This type of perception is called *the halo effect*. A person's initial positive impression of one thing, carries over to a similarly positive perception in the future—whether warranted, correct, or not. The reverse is also true regarding negative impressions. You should be careful about stereotypes affecting your perception. For example, people stereotype others based on ethnic background, age, sex, social status, and religion. A stereotype impression may lead to inaccurate and unfounded assumptions.

Confirmation bias is the tendency to interpret or look for evidence to confirm your own beliefs about something. Bias occurs even with the evidence of contradictory information. Bias is the systemic error of thought processing, whose effect is strengthened by emotion. People will interpret information or perceive things in a biased manner, to support their own beliefs or conclusions.

The anchoring effect is the tendency for you to evaluate, contrast, and compare only a limited number of factors. You tend to use a single value, consideration, or fact as the benchmark to compare everything else. A self-fulfilling prophecy occurs when you have expectations and you subconsciously set your environment and mind to fulfill them. These expectations may be positive or negative. If you think of yourself as a failure, you make little effort to complete a task, and your perception may be permanently altered. Just the opposite is true as well. Successful people believe in themselves and will positively perceive their environment.

It all depends on how we look at things and not how they are in themselves.

— Carl Jung

Change the way you look at things and the things you look at change. Fear distorts your perception and is usually more intense. It makes any distortion more pronounced. A person who is terribly afraid of snakes might mistake a piece of rope lying on the ground as a snake. Someone who is depressed tends to believe there is no hope or all hope is gone. Their perception will be dramatically different than when they were not depressed.

Other than Jesus who has perfect perception, a person who has legendary perception skills is Sherlock Holmes. During my internship, I spent two months on a cardiology rotation. The cardiologist I interned with was an exceptional doctor. He told me that if I wanted to be a great doctor, I needed to read some of the Sherlock Holmes books. He said it would improve my clinical skills and the ability to diagnose the problems in my patients. I read several of the books and agree that every doctor should read them.

I particularly like them because Arthur Conan Doyle wrote them. Dr. Doyle was an ophthalmologist born in 1859 in Edinburgh, Scotland. He studied medicine at the University of Edinburgh Medical School and studied ophthalmology in Vienna. He wrote many stories and books, but he is most famous for the Sherlock Holmes books. Arthur Doyle wrote four novels and 56 short stories about Sherlock Holmes. Dr. Joseph Bell inspired the Sherlock Holmes character.

Arthur Doyle met him at medical school where he was one of his professors. Dr. Bell made an indelible impression on Arthur Doyle. Dr. Doyle described Dr. Bell as a thin, wiry, dark man with a high-nosed acute face, penetrating grey eyes, and angular shoulders. Dr. Bell would sit in his receiving room with a red Indian face and diagnose the people as they came in, before they even opened their mouths. He would then give them details of their past life and would hardly ever make a mistake. Arthur Doyle dedicated The Adventures of Sherlock Holmes to Dr. Bell. Dr. Bell was Sherlock Holmes. Sherlock Holmes is famous for his precise perception and deductive reasoning. Here are a few of his famous quotes.

"The world is full of obvious things which nobody by chance ever observes."

"You see, but you do not observe. The distinction is clear."

"You know my method. It is founded upon observation of trifles."

"There is nothing more deceptive than an obvious fact."

"It is an old maxim of mine that when you have excluded the impossible, whatever remains however improbable, must be the truth."

Steven Covey said in his book, The 7 Habits of Highly Effective People, "To change ourselves effectively, we first had to change our perceptions."

Thomas Dewar stated, "Minds are like parachutes; they work best when open."

Let us look at the Bible and see what it says about perception, or another term would be *discernment*. Perception is a significant part of the teaching and guidance found in Scripture. There are approximately seven different Hebrew words in the Old Testament related to perception and eleven Greek words in the New Testament pertaining to perception.

There are two basic types of perception. There is the perception of things in the physical world and perception of things spiritually. Perception is about seeing things externally and internally. Perception is seeing beyond what is obvious and understanding the underlying reality. The challenge is to learn to develop perfect perception to live life in harmony with God's plan for your life.

Perfect perception results from training yourself to perceive the physical world, as well as the spiritual world.

> *Ultimate reality can best be realized with pure vision and perfect perception.*

> — James E. Croley III, M.D.

There are many Bible verses about Jesus perceiving.

Mark 2:8 NIV

Immediately Jesus knew in his spirit that this was what they were thinking in their hearts, and he said to them, "Why are you thinking these things?"

Perfect perception involves spiritual and physical perception. You often know what someone will say before they say it, because you know the person and their tendencies. Here is another example of Jesus perceiving.

Luke 5:22 NLT

Jesus knew what they were thinking, so he asked them, "Why do you question this in your hearts?"

Jesus used parables many times in His teachings. Jesus was masterful at telling stories. He used parables, analogies, and metaphors in His teachings to provide or convey truths in a more memorable and meaningful way. The word *parable* or *parables* appears in the four Gospels 45 times. A parable is a fictitious narrative of common life or earthly story with a heavenly meaning or spiritual truth. Jesus used parables to make truth relevant and practical. He also used parables to conceal the truth. It would be best if you had spiritual perception to understand the meaning of the parables. Parables captivate your attention and help you remember its teachings. Perfect perception is key to understanding God's Word and applying it to your life.

Mark 4:11-12 NLT

He replied, "You are permitted to understand the secret of the Kingdom of God. But I use parables for everything I say to outsiders, so that the Scriptures might be fulfilled: When they see what I do, they will learn nothing. When they hear what I say, they will not understand. Otherwise, they will turn to me and be forgiven."

1 John 2:15-17 NLT MSG

Don't love the world's ways. Don't love the world's goods. Love of the world squeezes out the love for the Father. Practically everything that goes on in the world—wanting your own way, wanting everything for yourself, wanting to appear important—has nothing to do with the Father. It just isolates you from him. The world and all its wanting, wanting, wanting is on the way out—but whoever does what God wants is set for eternity.

People do not have the correct perception, because they do not see through spiritual eyes or can see through the eyes of Jesus. Your database or paradigm keeps you from perceiving things as they really are. Perfect perception requires looking through a Christian or God-centered paradigm.

Job 32:8-9 NIV

But it is the spirit in a person, the breath of the Almighty that gives them understanding. It is not only the old who are wise, not only the aged who understand what is right.

Discernment is another way of looking at perception. Discernment is the ability to make a spiritual distinction or the ability to see beyond the obvious. Discernment helps to lead you, guide you, and protect you. When you face trials, how can you distinguish between what you believe is happening based on your limited perception, and what is truly happening from God's perspective? How can you trust human perceptions, observations, or feelings related to your perception, as the true reliable nature of what is real or what is not real? God tells you to trust in Him and not rely on your understanding.

Proverbs 3:5-6 NIV

Trust in the Lord with all your heart and lean not on your own understanding; in all your ways submit to him, and he will make your paths straight.

Psalm 37:3-7 NLT

Trust in the Lord and do good. Then you will live safely in the land and prosper. Take delight in the Lord, and he will give you your heart's desires. Commit everything you do to the Lord. Trust him, and he will help you. He will make your innocence radiate like the dawn, and the justice of your cause will shine like the noonday sun. Be still in the presence of the Lord, and wait patiently for him to act.

Perfect perception is not possible, but better perception is possible. You can teach an old dog new tricks. The mind is flexible and has tremendous plasticity that you can mold and change. Great perception will improve your relationship with God. You will see the path God has laid out for you from a new perspective. Without a God centered paradigm, you may not be able to perceive God acting in your life.

Job 9:11 NLT

Yet when he comes near, I cannot see him. When he moves by, I do not see him go.

Job 33:14 NLT

For God speaks again and again, though people do not recognize it.

Many people are unable to see or hear God in the world of today. Everyone is focused on themselves. They think their intelligence and technology are all that matters. People are addicted to their flat screens and are being directed by the propaganda on them. They are too busy to listen to God. The totalitarian mindset of today wishes to abolish God and the family from society. They should pay attention to the words of wisdom in the Bible.

Psalm 46:10 NLT

Be still and know that I am God!

Psalm 119:105 NLT

Your word is a lamp unto my feet and a light for my path.

Improved perception will improve you and the choices you make. You can learn to hear God's direction for your life. You can develop your physical and spiritual perception skills. Further in the book, I will show you how you can improve your perception. It will be a fun and exciting lesson.

A fool sees not the same tree that a wise man sees.

— William Blake

Your mind composes what you see—and you choose to see what you want to see.

— James E. Croley III, M.D.

Chapter 5
Flat Screens

1 John 2:15-17 NLT

Do not love this world nor the things it offers you, for when you love the world, you do not have the love of the Father in you. For the world offers only a craving for physical pleasure, a craving for everything we see, and pride in our achievements and possessions. These are not from the Father, but are from this world. And this world is fading away, along with everything that people crave. But anyone who does what pleases God will live forever.

At first glance, flat screens might sound like a weird title for a chapter in a Christian book. As I stated initially, your vision is the primary portal for sin to enter your life and how the secular world will control your thoughts and beliefs. I chose the title of this chapter as everyone's life is dominated by a flat screen of some size or type today. Flat screens dominate people's lives today.

A flat screen is any medium showing you a video, motion picture, providing you social media, or any screen that you spend time watching. The average American adult spends more than eleven hours a day looking at a flat screen of some kind. People are spending more than four hours a day on a computer, tablet, or smartphone. If you use a computer at work, the hours are higher.

People spend around five hours a day watching TV. Children age 8 to18 spend more than nine hours with some type of screen media. Today, the average adult consumes more than five times the information than adults did fifty years ago. Almost all that information is visual. This amount of information will alter the brain and how it processes all this data per day. The brain may have trouble analyzing and storing this amount of information. Mental health issues will be more likely to arise from the enormous amount of increased stimulation and brain activity. This brain stimulation will change how you think and how the brain organizes information.

Dopamine is a neurotransmitter or chemical messenger that sends information from one brain neuron to another brain cell. Dopamine is the primary neurotransmitter involved with the brain's reward system and feelings of pleasure. It is released into the brain when someone does something or sees something that warrants a reward, a pleasure response, or even when a person anticipates a reward. The rewards may include behaviors like drug use or sex.

The drug cocaine blocks the reuptake of dopamine—which means the brain is flooded with dopamine. This excess of dopamine leads to the euphoric feeling of using cocaine. The rush of dopamine experienced when using cocaine and other drugs causes the euphoria people feel, contributing to addiction. All of the flat screen activity releases dopamine, just like in drug addiction. High screen times increase the levels of dopamine which then overstimulates the brain. The brain becomes addicted to the flat screen in a similar way as drug addiction or any other addiction.

There is a new Silicone Valley fad called Dopamine Fasting. Even people in the social media business have realized what they are doing to their brains. Dr. Cameron Sepath, a clinical professor of psychiatry at the University of California, San Francisco, coined the term *dopamine fasting*. He recommends taking a break from behaviors that trigger strong amounts of dopamine release (especially in a repeated fashion) allowing the brain to recover and restore itself. Sepath believes that dopamine fasting is *the antidote to our overstimulated age*. The break could be an hour at the end of the day. You could consider taking a day away from all flat screens and technology on the weekend.

Some people use fasting time from flat screens to increase or renew their response when returning to their social media use. Constant flat screen use has dulled their reactions to what they are viewing. So, taking a break may help them get that thrill again, when they go online. Not everyone believes that Dopamine Fasting is valuable or lowers dopamine levels. Taking time out for mental rejuvenation is never a bad thing, but it is also nothing new. The intent behind Dopamine Fasting was to provide a rationale suggestion for disconnecting from days of technology-driven frenzy. It is substituting more simple activities to help people reconnect with themselves.

The Chinese government has decided that all flat screen use is not good for young boys and has limited its use. They can be on their flat screens for one hour on Friday, Saturday, and Sunday nights from eight to nine o'clock.

From the beginning, God told humankind to take one day of rest each week. God tells us to spend time with Him. Even before all the technology, He knew man needed rest.

Psalm 46:10 NLT

Be still, and know that I am God

We live in a visual world. There are not only beautiful natural things in this world, but images that humankind has made. The simple flat screen is a single frame image. You have heard that a picture paints a thousand words. Every day you are bombarded with thousands of single-frame photos. Things like billboards on the side of the road, images in social media, single-framed images on TV newscasts, newspapers, and magazines are in front of you all day long. Media, such as magazines and newspapers, are diminishing because of online technology. Artists created single-framed images in their drawings and paintings that portrayed a message.

Nicèphore Nièpce invented the first photograph in 1826. Since that time, these single-frame images have been everywhere. If you traveled back in time just a short while before photographs were invented and showed a picture to someone, they would think it was witchcraft.

The first flat screens developed for viewing were initially invented to entertain you, but they have advanced way beyond that today. Flat screens are used at work, in business software programs, schools, conference calls, webinars, movies, games, cars, alarm clocks, Facetime, read books, remote TV, music, study, research, emergency 911, and storage. The list could go on and on.

Many adults spend long hours working on a computer every day, but adults also consume large amounts of time on their smartphones, tablets, and TV. Technology dictates the way you learn and live life. How is this going to affect the health of your brain over time? The answer is still out, but early evidence indicates that it is altering the mind and how the brain processes data. Teens are showing higher rates of depression and loneliness, as they spend more time on their smartphones. Bullying is much more prevalent through social media than in the past.

New studies show that flat screens alter the brains of infants and young children. The American Academy of Pediatrics suggests that flat screens should be avoided in children under 24 months of age. Children ages two to five should be limited to one hour a day watching flat screens. There is a relationship between screen time in children and body-mass index, less sleep per night, delays in cognition, language development, and social-emotional development.

Recently the JAMA Pediatrics published a study titled, *Association Between Screen-Based Media Use and Brain White Matter Integrity in Preschool-Aged Children*. This study suggests that more flat-screen time meant lower expressive language, decreased literacy skills, and less ability to name objects rapidly. There were also physical changes in brain structure. It had significantly lower brain white matter integrity related to language and literacy skills in a portion of the brain. Now, this was a small study. More research is needed. The NIH is doing an extensive research project of 12,000 children in a ten-year study to get better answers.

In my practice of ophthalmology, I see teenagers with significant dry eye problems. In the past, dry eye disease only occurred in older people. When people stare at a flat screen, they decrease their blinking rate and the eye begins to dry out. Children are spending hours playing video games. Their blinking rates are low, as they do not want to miss a single second of the action. I recommend that playing time should be limited to one hour at a time. They need to take a break. After playing or staring at a flat screen for an hour or so, it is also a good idea to put a drop of artificial tears in the eyes.

Let us look at flat screens and see how we got to where we are today. The first flat screen for viewing images was the movie theater. In the beginning, the movie theaters were developed for entertainment, but it did not take long before they were used for other purposes. The first commercially public showing of a movie was the Lumière brothers' short film shown in Paris on December 28, 1895. The movie was called *The Arrival of the Train*. The movie was about a train approaching the station. It is rumored that it scared the people in the audience, causing chaos. It was designed to produce a reaction by the audience. Production companies were established all around the world very soon afterward.

The earliest films were black and white and under one minute in length, which is a far cry from the movies today. In 1897, the first film studios were built. The State Theater in Washington, Iowa is the oldest continuously operating movie theater in the world. In the 1920s, the United States reached its most significant film production era, producing 800 films annually. Until 1927, motion pictures were produced without sound. A pianist or musician sometimes accompanied the motion pictures. In 1927, Warner released the movie, *The Jazz Singer*, which had sound in portions of the movie. By 1929, almost all films contained sound.

Movie producers continued to develop new and better ways of entertaining people. Editing became important, so they could present things exactly as they wanted them portrayed. In 1935, Technicolor was invented and color pictures were born. Drive-in movies became a new way of going to the movies. Film continued to advance with the development of 3-D movies. Then Disney took movies to another experience level—4-D movies. Disney added the sensation of smell and the motion of your seat to increase the experience.

As I said early on, people realized how much movies could influence people watching films. Watching flat screens has the power to control even the very smartest people. The human mind is incredibly susceptible to the effects of watching movies, videos, and other social media. The conscious and subconscious brain absorbs all the visual stimuli your eyes are observing. All images, even some that you may not wish to remember, are stored. The more important or significant images are more prevalent in your memory.

Movie producers did not know it at the time, but they were trying to stimulate the emotional portion of the brain or limbic system. By stimulating the brain, they could change the way people think and believe.

Companies wanting to sell their products know that flat screens are the best way to entice you to buy their products. Stalin and Hitler realized the power of movies and used the flat screen to their advantage. Very quickly, the first flat screen became a propaganda medium to control the people. Unfortunately, people are still being influenced by what they see on a flat screen.

In 1896, the Lumière brothers went to Saint Petersburg. They showed their movies to a small Russian audience. In that same year, the Russian film industry produced a film showing the coronation of what would turn out to be the last monarch. The Bolsheviks would revolutionize the Russian film industry, as its leaders recognized the potential of film propaganda to influence the people's political views and social culture. Vladimir Lenin understood the power of movies when he stated, "Of all the arts, for us, cinema is the most important."

Propaganda films have been used throughout history. Lenin regarded the film industry in terms of its effectiveness. He promoted propaganda that would appeal to Russia's primarily illiterate people. Stalin acted as the ultimate censor. He ordered the cutting of films, films to be remade or destroyed. Stalin suggested subjects and genres, directors, writers, actors, and composers. He read all the scripts before the movies were produced. Film offered something beyond what pamphlets, photos, or posters could offer—realism or real-life stories.

The Bolsheviks controlled the film industry and produced movies that promoted communist themes around Russia. Under the direction of Joseph Stalin (until he died in 1953) movies focused on the Bolsheviks version of history—enshrining the ideals of the revolution, promoting international revolution, calling on all workers to unite against any oppressors, celebrating Stalin as a great leader, and justifying any means necessary to protect the people.

The Soviet film industry developed a uniform style known as *socialist realism*. The propaganda movies were shown from city to city and in the countryside. Movies were transported by trains around the countryside and were shown in railway stations, indoctrinating everyone to the Communist way of life. They went to the people, as they wanted everyone to believe the propaganda in the films.

Famous Russian producer Sergei Eisenstein mastered the editing and sound precisely, to make the audience sense panic and fear. In the film October, Eisenstein portrayed the Bolsheviks in the highest regard. He portrayed them as righteous revolutionaries with the people's mandate to overthrow the government. Through Stalin's leadership, the propaganda movies promoted class enemy struggles. The message was clear—the religious elites and Western capitalists were oppressors of the unpretentious working class. Sheila Fitzpatrick said:

The kind of renunciation that most interested Soviet authorities was when priests renounced the cloth. Such renunciation, if done publicly, provided dramatic support for the Soviet position, that religion was a fraud that had been discredited by modern science.

Through the dramatic and vivid power of movies, great filmmakers promoted the policies of the Communist Party to audiences throughout Russia.

Hitler and the Nazis were very aware of movies' propagandistic effects during the beginning of their rise in Germany. Hitler created an elaborate system of propaganda through the use of film. Hitler and his propaganda minister, Joseph Goebbels, were movie fans. The use of cinema for propaganda was planned by the National Socialist German Workers Party in 1930. They made cinema a department in the party. Joseph Goebbels bombarded the German people with propaganda associating Jews with rats. After years of this propaganda, the German people developed a subconscious association of Jews with rats. Nazism influenced the masses by employing slogans aimed at the emotions of the people. Hitler thought films would have enormous power and influence in promoting his propaganda. Hitler wrote about the psychological effects of images in <u>Mein Kampf</u>:

> *One must also remember that of itself the multitude is mentally inert. That it remains attached to its old habits and that it is not naturally prone to read something which does not conform with its own pre-established beliefs when such writing does not contain what the multitude hopes to find there...*

> *The picture, in all its forms, including the film, has better prospects. ... In a much shorter time, at one stroke I might say, people will understand a pictorial presentation of something which it would take them a long time and laborious effort of reading to understand.*

Nazi propagandist Hans Traub, who earned his PhD in a dissertation on the press, wrote the essay, "The Film as a Political Instrument," in 1932:

> *Without any doubt the film is a formidable means of propaganda. Achieving propagandistic influence has always demanded a 'language' which forms a memorable and passionate plot with a simple narrative. ... In the vast area of such 'language' that the recipients are directly confronted by in the course of technical and economical processes, the most effective is the moving picture. It demands permanent alertness; it's full of surprises concerning the change of time, space, and action; it has an unimaginable richness of rhythm for intensifying or dispelling emotions.*

Joseph Goebbels appointed himself the "Patron of the German film." Goebbels nationalized film production and distribution. Joseph Goebbels stated:

If you tell a lie big enough and keep repeating it, people will come to believe it.

It is not propaganda's task to be intelligent, its task is to lead to success.

Propaganda works best when those who are being manipulated are confident that they are acting on their own free will.

The Nazis could control and manipulate the people. The Nazis showed movies in military barracks and factories. They operated three hundred film trucks and two film trains to expand their influence into Germany's rural areas. Just like Stalin, they wanted everyone exposed to their propaganda. Ninety percent of communication is visual—and the Nazis and Russians used it to their advantage.

The next flat screen to appear on the market was the television or TV. Companies, politicians, anyone who wants to sell you something, or anyone who wants to influence you, wants to be in your life as many hours a day as possible. So the TV brought movies, entertainment, news, and many other programs right into your living room. Everyone wants your attention and to occupy more of your time.

The first TV model was a twelve-inch screen that cost $445 or the equivalent of $8,083 in 2019. The TV became popular after World War II. The first color television was on the scene in 1953. Only 0.5% of U.S. households had a television in 1946, 55.7%

in 1954, and over 90% by 1962. Today's LCD TVs are huge. Many households have turned their family room into a theater at home with stereo surround sound. You have a theater at home to stimulate your mind and increase the effectiveness of the programs you are watching.

The next flat screen sold to the public created a monumental and everlasting change in how people live their lives. It is the computer. Adding a computer's capabilities to a flat screen allows society to connect with one another—no matter where in the world they reside. Companies were able to develop software to control almost everything done in our routine daily lives, in addition to the shortlist at the beginning of this chapter. The personal computer industry began in 1977 with the introduction of Apple's computer (Apple II), Tandy Radio Shack's computer (TRS-80), Commodore Business Machines' computer, and the Personal Electronic Transactor (PET). The IBM Corporation, the world's dominant computer maker, did not produce the IBM Personal Computer until 1981. By the 1990s, some personal computers were small enough to be portable. Smaller and lighter computers would eventually lead to a flat screen being with you nearly 24 hours a day.

In 1983, instead of naming a person of the year, Time Magazine named the computer the Machine of the Year. That is how important they viewed the personal computer. The internet would take connectivity and your involvement with a flat screen each day to a new level. The number of internet hosts reaches 1,000 in 1984—100,000 in 1989—1,000,000 in 1992—10,000,000 in 1996—and by 2001 the number had reached 100,000,000.

On September 4, 1998, Google appeared on the scene. Can you imagine living without being able to search for something on

Google? In 1994, Amazon.com was founded and changed how people shop. In 2004, Mark Zuckerberg developed Facebook, and the beginning of social media began.

As technology advanced, the flat-screen devices became smaller. The smaller, lighter tablet computer used a touch screen display. The computer gets even smaller with the ultra-mobile PC, and then down to a pocket PC.

As technology advances, the retinal display makes it possible for the iPad and smartphones to be useable. Apple released the iPad in 2010. The tablet would become popular because of its size and portability. The iPad or other tablet computers can always be with you. By May of 2017, Apple had sold more than 360 million iPads.

How would Hitler look at flat screens today? He would be salivating at the opportunity of how he could easily change the world. Flat screens are everywhere in society today. You do not need to have people go to a theater to project your propaganda. When the antichrist arrives, he will not have any problem getting the masses to follow him.

The next evolution in flat screens was the smartphone. Before I discuss smartphone development, I would like to give you information about the newest flat screen, the smartwatch. You can now wear a flat screen on your wrist!

In 2013, the first-ever smartwatch with the full capability of a smartphone was launched. Apple Inc. brought it to the market on September 9, 2014. Samsung unveiled its smartwatch, the Samsung Gear S2, in October of 2015. The smartwatch is a wearable computer in the form of a wristwatch with a touchscreen interface. These watches may include a digital camera, thermometers, pedometers, heart rate monitors, GPS receivers, barometers, compasses, tiny speakers, digital maps, schedulers, personal organizers, calculators, and other software apps. Astonishingly, you can do all these things from a wristwatch today. It is still too early to tell whether it will become more popular than the smartphone.

Smartphones are the dominant flat screen today. Smartphones perform the same functions as the smartwatch, plus many more applications. The larger screen allows you to do many more tasks and has an unlimited number of applications. It is just like a laptop computer that fits in your pocket. It is way more than just a phone.

Since the unveiling of the iPhone in 2007, most smartphones feature multi-touch touchscreens instead of keyboards. They download or purchase a wide variety of applications from a centralized store and use cloud storage, virtual assistants, email functions, texting, and mobile payment options. You can do almost anything with your smartphone. Today's smartphone has 30,000 times the processing speed of the 70 pound navigational computer on Apollo 11 that guided the mission landing on the moon in 1969!

Time Magazine named the computer the Machine of the Year in 1982. Time Magazine also named the smartphone the most influential gadget of all time. It has fundamentally changed our interaction with technology. Smartphones have changed the way everyone lives their lives today. People are addicted to their smartphones.

There was a study on TV where they took the phones away from several young ladies for two weeks, to see how they would react to not having their phones. Their anxiety levels were extremely high. A couple of them felt they were on the verge of a nervous breakdown. They did not do well without their phones.

Personal communication through a device is now the preferred way of communication. People do not want to speak in person to one another. Young people today are not comfortable talking directly to someone. Society or culture is drastically changing because of flat-screen technology.

Are Christians using technology to transform the world or is technology transforming Christians in unhealthy ways?

— George M. Marden

The average American looks at their smartphone 96 times a day. Americans are looking at their phones 15 billion times a day! Are we preoccupied with these flat screens today? It is pretty obvious!

Smartphones are at the top of the league in most used flat-screen devices.

- Virtual reality headsets 8%
- Smartwatches 15%
- Fitness bands 21%
- Desktop computers 57%
- Laptop computers 77%
- Smartphones 94%

You tap, swipe, and click on your smartphone 2,617 times a day. You send or receive a text 94 times a day. Seventy five percent of Americans use their smartphones on the toilet! You are going to use them everywhere, right! Eighty-seven percent of millennials say that their smartphones never leave their side. The average American spends 5.4 hours on their smartphone a day, which is a total of 67 days a year. It is difficult to imagine that you spend 67 days a year on your smartphone! Teens spend nearly eight hours a day on a smartphone, and children ages 8 to 12 spend almost five hours a day. The prevalence of using a flat screen is one of the primary reasons for writing this book. Flat screens and social media dominate social interaction, which is especially true for young people today. Socially and culturally, technology is changing the world. You and I will relate differently to one another. It can also change how the world relates to God.

Unhealthy flat-screen addictions are flourishing because people do not see the consequences. Facebook, Instagram, YouTube, Snap Chat, and other smartphone apps distract you from the world around you. Many times, these apps become a way of escaping from reality or dealing with society's turmoil. The news cycle is 24 hours a day. There is instant access to news. The culture today is all about me, and I want instant gratification. Americans live a hectic life with flat screens pouring out information all day long.

Your smartphone is continually going off to let you know if you have a text message, your next appointment, a new email— or you receive a phone call for which you have different ring tones for other people. These unchecked distractions can make it challenging to listen to God's Holy Spirit trying to communicate with you. Distraction management is becoming a necessary skill that everyone needs to become more diligent in doing. All this stress of technology or flat screens will take its toll on the health and well-being of people.

Everyone wants immediate responses and approval for everything in their lives. We live in the now generation. Smartphones are contributing to this need or addiction for immediate self-gratification. People are reading fewer books, because there is not enough action or stimulation. Millennials think this way. They are not likely going to read the Bible. Tweets, snaps, texts, games, and YouTube are the critical thing in their lives.

You may be unaware, but everything you do online is monitored. Google's spiders know every page you have looked at and know how long you were on that page. There are software programs and website companies that businesses can pay to follow you, once you have clicked on a page related to their business. You will keep seeing their ad or website as you search the internet, in order to entice you to buy or go to their website. The companies pay a fee for following you for thirty days at a time. Google will show you pages you might be interested in, based on the pages you have been on in the past. Big Tech has studied your search patterns and knows the things that will interest you. Google will send you a conglomerate of websites, images, and advertisements. They are packaged to stimulate you to watch, buy, or influence the way they want you to think. They want to keep you excited, thrilled, and craving the time you spend on your smartphone.

By stimulating your brain's limbic system on your smartphone, you become more addicted to its whims and fantasies. Your brain becomes addicted to the feelings caused by the dopamine released in your brain. These are the same chemicals and areas of the brain as being addicted to drugs.

Smartphone time continues to increase each year. The words, images, videos, games, and other applications transform you over time. The vast amount of data your brain is receiving each day will keep changing you in the manner they desire. Your paradigm will begin to shift by the things you observe on your smartphone and other flat screens. If not careful, this stimulation will lead you further from God.

The increased use of flat screens begins to isolate you—you spend time alone watching the screen. Americans are becoming obese because of diet, little exercise, and outdoor activity. The flat screen started as a cinema where you got out of the house. Many times you went to the movie with other people. Flat screens isolate you—and Satan loves technology. He supports anything that takes your focus away from Jesus. Satan not only tempts you with big temptations, but probably works harder filling your mind with stuff through a flat screen. Spending hours aimlessly going from one screen to the next, thinking you are in control of your life when in actuality, you are addicted to the flat screen. How much time do you spend on a flat screen relating to God? You pay way more attention to the flat screen than spending time with the Holy Spirit. As I am saying all these things, I am just as guilty as you. Nearly all of us are addicted to flat screens.

I am going to share with you some facts that most of you will find shocking. Porn sites receive more regular traffic than Netflix, Amazon, and Twitter combined each month! Thirty-five percent of all downloads are porn-related. The porn industry globally is a 97 billion dollar business—and twelve billion in the United States. There are 52,560,000 minutes in 100 years or a century. Over 6,600 centuries of time was consumed on one of the largest porn sites in 2019 alone. The world's largest free porn site received over 42,000,000,000 site visits during 2019.

Young people ages 13 to 24 actively seek out pornography weekly or more often. Teenage girls are significantly more likely to seek out porn than women over age 25. The teen porn category has topped site searches for the last seven years. The number of child porn traders online in the United States is over 600,000.

All that information is mind-boggling! As I said in the beginning, sin first enters your mind through the eyes. It is essential in young people, as their brains are still maturing and growing, that screen time is limited. All this type of stimulation is going to alter how their minds think, function, and develop.

It is not just the mental aspects of long periods of screen time, but it also takes a physical toll. Sitting in front of a flat screen leads to obesity, dry eyes, eye fatigue, neck problems, thumb or finger problems from texting, increased stress, anxiety, poor posture-related problems, and sleeplessness—to name a few. Frequent users of flat screens have two to three times the risk of sleep disturbances. Checking your smartphone before you go to bed can be harmful. The next thing you know, it is 2 AM, and you are still looking at that screen. You experience information overload right before you are trying to go to sleep. If you keep your smartphone close by in the bedroom, you are being awakened by tweets, beeps, and other noises. You are looking at a bright screen right before trying to sleep, which alters your natural sleep cycle.

Smartphones should be put away at least one hour before going to bed. Keep them as far away as possible, but close enough that you can still hear it if it rings. Try reading a book. This book might be your best sleep medicine!

Flat screens have increased traffic accidents from people texting while driving. People walk into dangerous situations, as they are not watching where they are walking. Unfortunately, many people have died from their screen addiction.

Peter gives us great advice in the New Testament.

2 Peter 1:3-9 NLT

By his divine power, God has given us everything we need for living a godly life. We have received all of this by coming to know him, the one who called us to himself by means of his marvelous glory and excellence. And because of his glory and excellence, he has given us great and precious promises. These are the promises that enable you to share his divine nature and escape the world's corruption caused by human desires. In view of all this, make every effort to respond to God's promises. Supplement your faith with a generous provision of moral excellence, and moral excellence with knowledge, and knowledge with self-control, and self-control with patient endurance, and patient endurance with godliness, and godliness with brotherly affection, and brotherly affection with love for everyone. The more you grow like this, the more productive and useful you will be in your knowledge of our Lord Jesus Christ. But those who fail to develop in this way are shortsighted or blind, forgetting that they have been cleansed from their old sins.

Flat screens and technology are not going to disappear. Flat screens are going to advance and progress continually. Society is going to be transformed from where it was just a generation before. You may have seen different movies portraying the future, where people have lost all emotion, social interaction and appear almost like robots. Is that what the future holds for us? What new technology is going to influence the lives of people in the future? Will the flat screens of the future be connected right into our brain's limbic system? Will the stimulation be so intense that everyone will spend all their time connected to a flat screen? Maybe we will voluntarily hook ourselves up to technology, like in the movie The Matrix. What new technology is going to be available in the future?

OLED Displays

OLED displays can produce astounding high-resolution images on screens. OLED screens are already in use in smartphones and televisions. OLED displays may take over the entire screen industry. OLED displays are faster, thinner, and more energy-efficient than other technologies. OLED can be made very thin, transparent, and bendable. OLED displays may be in window glass or textiles. OLED displays have no inherent limitations to size and resolution. Eventually, there will be a gigantic TV in the living room, or a whole wall in the room could be a TV screen. Add a surround system, and you are better than a movie theater.

Your smartphone is going to change. They will have screens that roll out or unfold to have a much larger screen. OLED displays will open entirely new developments and markets.

There is a company called Mirror Inc. They make is nearly full-length mirror that shows you a workout video—and you can see yourself in the mirror, as well. You can see yourself following the workout with the instructor.

Haptic Touchscreens

Touchscreens burst onto the scene in smartphones and tablets in a noticeably short time. What is next in the touchscreen realm? It is a screen that touches you back! You will receive tactile sensations back from the screen surface. The screen surface dynamically changes while you are using it. The screen will send you sensations of a keyboard and surface textures, such as smooth or rough. Low electrical currents supply the sensations back to you. Maybe you will put on a bodysuit and electrical impulses will give the flat screen's life-like sensation. You will feel like you are in the middle of the action.

Virtual Reality or Augmented Reality

Oculus rift is a 3D head-mounted virtual reality display with motion tracking. The unit monitors your movements in response to what is displayed. Virtual reality displays will continue to advance. The Unreal Engine, paired with the Oculus Rift, will be an exponential leap in realism. Augmented reality is a concept where you add to the visual information on top of the real world. One form of augmented reality is Google's Project Glass system. A pair of glasses has a small camera attached to it. It could project directions for you to follow to a destination, give you information about a destination, or give you information on anything you may ask. It had great applications for the blind or visually impaired, as it could read a book or provide whatever information was needed. Google took it off the market because of complaints about privacy. Hopefully, it will continue to be available for the blind.

Glasses-Free 3D

3D Movies and 3D TVs require 3D glasses to see three dimensionally. People watching a 3D TV in their homes do not like having to wear 3D glasses. New technology will produce 3D displays or cinema screens that do not require 3D glasses.

Holographic Displays

Remember the Star Wars scene where R2-D2 projected a hologram image of a glowing Princess Leia desperately asking

Obi-Wan for help. The Holodeck on Star Trek is where the person could experience different virtual reality scenarios programmed into a computer. Maybe someday there will be an empty room in everyone's house called the Holoroom, where you could program any type of experience you desire. People may never leave the room!

My daughter teaches special needs kids in middle school. She can tell which kids spend all their time on flat screens with little parent interaction, from the other kids who spend quality time with their parents. Technology is producing a radical change in human behaviors. Where this will end is impossible to predict.

> *You don't need to go far to see hatred and abuse that happens online. Even using social media is anti-social because people are always on their phones.*
>
> — Ronny Chieng

> *Our attention spans have been reduced by the immediate gratification provided by smartphones and social media.*
>
> — Katherine Ryan

This ability to instantly see events happening around the world 24 hours a day may have been predicted in the Bible. In Revelation, there is an event that is observed by the whole world. God could miraculously reveal the event to everyone—or this event could not happen until the world's technology was available to see it.

Revelation 11:7-10 NLT

> *When they complete their testimony, the beast that comes up out of the bottomless pit will declare war against them, and he will conquer them and kill them. And their bodies will lie in the main street of Jerusalem, the city that is*

figuratively called "Sodom" and "Egypt", the city where their Lord was crucified. And for three and a half days, all peoples, tribes, languages, and nations will stare at their bodies. No one will be allowed to bury them. All the people who belong to this world will gloat over them and give presents to each other to celebrate the death of the two prophets who tormented them.

Unless God creates a miracle where everyone will see the two prophets, the technology of flat screens will allow viewing the prophets around the world. Flat screens and technology have many sensational aspects to how they interact in your life. They also have many negative aspects to living your life. It is especially true for children and young adults while their brains are developing. Personal social interaction should be encouraged. Children need to spend good quality time with their parents and with other children their age. Their flat screen time should be limited, filters should be placed on their devices to protect them from seeing unwanted material, and you should monitor what they are watching.

You remember the story of the Pied Piper. He wore a coat of many bright colors or pied clothing, which is the reason for his name. The bright-colored coat was part of his marketing scheme. You recall that he claimed to be a rat catcher. He promised the people of Hamelin, Germany, he would rid the city of all its rats and mice for a sum of money—as they were suffering from The Plague. The city agreed to the deal.

The Pied Piper took out a fife or small shrill flute and began to play. All the rats and mice left every house in town and gathered around him and his flute. The rats and the mice were mesmerized.

They all blindly followed him to the River Weser. He waded into the water. They followed him and drowned.

The citizens had been freed from the Plague. Now they regretted promising him so much money. So they refused to pay him. He went away bitter and angry. He returned dressed in a hunter's costume, wearing a bright red hat. He started playing his flute. This time, instead of the rats and mice running to him, all the children in town swarmed around him. They, too, were mesmerized and, in a zombie-like fashion, followed him into the mountains, never to be seen again.

The flat screens are societies Pied Piper of today. Children and young adults are mesmerized by playing games or watching their flat screens. They are becoming lost right in front of their parents' eyes and may never return from their addiction to the images they are watching. The imagery portrayed is strategically designed to control and alter the mind. The Pied Piper or flat screen has them and will not relinquish control easily.

God designed us to be socially active on a personal basis. A flat screen does not contribute to healthy social interaction. The constant use of these devices will alter your mind, as you become addicted to flat screens. The amount of information blasting your senses and mind each day will have consequences. Your vision, perception, and sense of reality will miss the whole point of your existence on earth. You will become blinded watching flat screens and only see what you have been programmed to see!

Satan loves the flat screen! He wants you to fill your mind with insignificant minutia and is in favor of anything that will keep you occupied. Satan is going to promote anything that keeps your mind away from God. He does not need to tempt you with a big sin. He will keep you fixated on social media and work on many little sins working his way up to a big one. All Satan must do is addict you to a flat screen. Satan is the great deceiver!

2 Corinthian 4:4 NLT

Satan, who is the god of this world, has blinded the minds of those who don't believe. They are unable to see the glorious light of the Good News. They don't understand this message about the glory of Christ, who is the exact likeness of God.

The eye is the portal that sin takes to enter your soul. Be careful about your flat-screen use! Satan never stops his effort to influence you!

Chapter 6
Cultural and Societal Paradigms

Revelation 7:9 NLT

After this I saw a vast crowd, too great to count, from every nation and tribe and people and language, standing in front of the throne and before the Lamb.

Galatians 3:26-29 NLT

For you are all children of God through faith in Christ Jesus. And all who have been united with Christ in baptism have put on Christ, like putting on new clothes. There is no longer Jew or Gentile, slave or free, male and female. For you are all one in Jesus Christ. And now that you belong to Christ, you are the true children of Abraham. You are his heirs, and God's promise to Abraham belongs to you.

Culture and society are rapidly changing compared to the centuries before. Before I get into discussing culture and societal paradigms, what is culture? The word *culture* is derived from the Latin word *colere,* which means *to tend to the earth, grow, cultivate, or nurture.* Culture is the characteristics of a group of people encompassing religion, beliefs, laws, customs, social habits, arts, music, language, cuisine, shared attitudes, goals, patterns of behavior, interactions between people, and cognitive constructs. Culture is composed of the type of clothes you wear, the kind of food you eat, your marriage, the music you listen to, how you greet another person, your family unit's makeup, the religion you practice, your perception or paradigm, and many other characteristics. Culture is the way you understand yourself—as an individual and a member of society.

Society is *a group of people with a common geographical location, community, or nation; a broad group of people having common traditions, institutions, collective activities, and interests.*

The United States is different from many other countries, as it is a pluralist society with many cultures and races. As a whole, we are Americans. When 9-11 happened, nearly 100% of Americans supported the president and the government. At other times, Americans are divided as to their beliefs and cultures. Societies construct patterns of behavior by deeming specific actions, opinions, or speech as acceptable or unacceptable. Society is a group of people and the relationships between the people and the institutions within the group.

Culture and society are intricately related. A culture consists of the characteristics of a society. Culture is different from society, in that it adds meaning to relationships. A society consists of people in a geographical location, who share a common culture or cultures. Thus, culture includes many societal aspects. Globalization is changing the relationship between culture and society.

Social norms in society are beliefs held by a group of people, implying how behavior should be in a given context. Cultural and societal parameters are in a stage of continuous and rapid change. For many centuries, a grandfather was not any different than a grandson. They thought, acted, and lived life in a remarkably similar manner.

For many centuries, humankind could be grouped into three categories. They were either hunter-gatherers, pastoralists, or horticulturalists.

The hunter-gatherer lived a life based on gathering wild plants and hunting animals. Typically, the man would hunt the animals and the women would gather the plants. Hunter-gatherer societies tend to live nomadic lives with low-density populations.

The pastoralist lives primarily utilizing domesticated livestock. The horticulturalists live primarily by means of cultivating crops. This society allows for an increased density of population and food surplus, for selling or trading with others.

Man lived as one of the three groups for generation after generation, with little change in culture or society. It was not until industry came on the scene that humanity significantly changed its way of life.

An industrial society's primary means of living is working in industry. Industry focused on the manufacturing of goods. They lived in more densely populated areas. Where relationships in pre-industrial societies were more likely to develop at church or proximity of housing, an industrial society brings people together with similar occupations.

The post-industrial society arrives on the scene in which the primary means of living is service-oriented work. Technology pops into existence, causing significant and rapid changes in America's cultural and societal characteristics, compared to the centuries before. Now each generation has its title and set of new characteristics and beliefs.

The generations of the first half of the 20th century were very similar in their beliefs and lifestyle. There were just a few small differences between them.

The Lost Generation was a cohort of people that came of age during World War I. They were described as being disoriented, wandering, and directionless. My grandfather was a member of that generation and he was nothing like that description. He knew exactly what he wanted in life and, through determination, became successful. I do not think that my grandfather, father, or I are very different from one another.

The Silent Generation refers to people born between 1925 and 1945. The children who grew up during this time worked very hard and kept quiet.

The Greatest Generation is also known as the G.I. Generation or World War II Generation. This generation was born between the years of 1901 to 1927. Tom Brokaw popularized the term *Greatest Generation*. This generation came out of the hardships of the Great Depression and won World War II. They knew how to survive and solve problems.

There were still small differences in these generations. The next generations started to have different beliefs and characteristics.

The crucial differences which distinguish human societies and human beings are not biological. They are cultural.

— Ruth Benedict

Baby Boomers were born between 1944 and 1964. There are 76 million Baby Boomers in the United States. Baby Boomers were the first generation to have a flat screen or TV in their homes. Baby Boomers are characterized by a strong work ethic, self-assured, competitive, goal-oriented, mentally focused, team-oriented, and disciplined. Baby boomers have a high divorce rate and second marriages. They are ambitious, can handle a crisis, have good communication skills, hesitant about taking too much time off work, anxious to please, will go the extra mile, and speak openly and directly.

The next generations have grown up with computers, computer games, smartwatches, and smartphones. Each generation spends more time on these devices—and social media becomes more critical with each generation.

Generation X people were born between 1965 and 1980. The X generation people are called the latchkey kids and were raised by dual-income families or single parents. Their values include balance, diversity, highly educated, high job expectations, and a lack of organizational loyalty. They may be angry, but do not know why. They are independent, have a strong sense of entitlement, and ignore leadership.

Women are widely expected to work outside the home. They wish to have a balance between work and family after watching their workaholic parents. They enjoy work, but are more concerned about work/life navigation. They dislike rigid work requirements and want the latest technology. They use email as their number one tool—and talk is in short bites.

Generation Y, or commonly known as Millennials, were born between 1981 and 2000. The term *Millennials* was first introduced by Neil Howe and William Strauss in their book Generations. A known American sociologist, Kathleen Shaputis, labeled this

Millennials group as the *Peter Pan Generation*. They are also known as the *Boomerang Generation*, because the Millennial's perceived tendency was to delay some rites of passage into adulthood for more extended periods than previous generations. They are digital media children and grew up as children of divorced parents.

If current trends continue, Millennials will have a lower marriage rate than previous generations. More than half of Millennials do not plan to have children. They are the first generation to have schedules. Their values are diversity, members of a global community, incredibly tech-savvy, intensely spiritual but not religious, avid consumers, and self-confident. They are attached to their technology gadgets, have not lived without a computer, are ambitious but not focused, have a global way of thinking, high-speed stimulus junkies, and like to think outside the box. They are coddled kids, as everyone got a trophy just for participating. They are effective workers, but are out the door at 5 PM on the dot. They like flex time, job sharing, and sabbaticals. They believe that technology allows them to work flexibly, anyplace, and should be evaluated on work product—not when or where they got it done. They expect to work with positive people and companies that fulfill their dreams. They want to be treated with respect despite their age and expect to get paid well. They lack skills for dealing with difficult people, lack discipline, need structure, and need supervision. They do not like being talked down to and will resent being thought of as inferior, just because they are younger.

Javelin Research has studied this group and believe that not all Millennials are in the same life stages. They have decided that Generation Y should be divided into Generation Y.1 and

Generation Y.2. Culture and society are changing so rapidly that we are dividing a single generation into two groups. According to Javelin Research, the two groups are culturally different.

Generation Z people were born from 1995 to 2020. This group is also known as iGeneration, Post-millennials, Zoomers, and Homeland Generation. Generation Z people are more racially and ethnically diverse than any other generation. They are going to be the most well-educated generation yet. Generation Zs received their first smartphone by age 10. Many of them have grown up using their own smartphones or their parents' smartphones or tablets at an exceedingly early age. They are growing up in a hyper-connected world. The smartphone is their preferred piece of technology. This generation has observed the struggle and debt of Millennials and is more conservative financially. They prefer debit cards over credit cards. The two generations of Z and Y have many similar opinions on the major issues of today. Ideas about gender are rapidly changing in the world and Generation Z is at the forefront of it. America now needs to use gender-neutral pronouns. This generation is going further away from God.

We have reached the end of the alphabet and society or culture is changing rapidly. Do we start back at the beginning of the alphabet? The experts in sociology will make the decision. As we go from Generation X to Z, there is a significant religious association trend, with the upcoming generations being less religious.

A new culture has emerged out of nowhere and is not related to the year you are born. It is called the Cancel Culture. The beginning of the Cancel Culture started with the political correctness movement in the 1970s. Many people downplayed political correctness and thought it was just a short-lived unimportant fad.

Political correctness was used by left-wing activists in various new social movements. Political correctness is *to choose words or actions that avoid offending, disparaging, or have insulting meaning to groups of oppressed people*. The backlash began in the 1990s. Conservatives began using the term *political correctness* to criticize the left for imposing their views on others and suppressing dissenting opinions. Politically correct language is selective on who or what group arbitrarily deserves more respect. Many people felt that political correctness had gone too far. The words being banned would only be thought offensive by only hyper-alert people with an agenda. Here are some examples: Forefathers—now only ancestors. Chairman or Chairwoman—now only chairperson. Slum—now only economically deprived area. Right-hand man—now only chief assistant

Political correctness was the precursor to the Cancel Culture. Cancel Culture is a modern form of ostracism. If you do not like someone or what they have said, you can thrust them out of society or professional circles. Civil discussion or deliberation about important subjects, that may be controversial about social or political topics, is vanishing from the American landscape. Eighty-five percent of college students report that they have stopped expressing opinions on sensitive issues to avoid offending someone. All kinds of people are being canceled.

President George Washington and Thomas Jefferson have been canceled from society. Christopher Columbus is now a bad person and has been canceled. Florida State University removed the statue of Francis Eppes VII, who was the former mayor of Tallahassee and grandson of Thomas Jefferson. J.K. Rowling, author of the Harry Potter series, has been canceled. Disney cites racist portrayals in its movies Dumbo, Peter Pan, Swiss Family Robinson, and The AristoCats. They have been removed from their list of movies for young children. Six of Dr. Seuss's books have been removed from publication for apparent racial undertones. Mike Lindell of My Pillow has been canceled. Pepe Le Pew was a serial sexual harasser and normalized rape culture. Dove soap is removing the word *normal* from its product advertising, as the word *normal* may make some people feel excluded. Abraham Lincoln was a racist and needed to be removed from history! The list is very long of the things canceled in America.

Without the knowledge of history, humankind is doomed to repeat the same mistakes. Some people wish to cancel America, because it is so horrible. By canceling tangible reminders of all the aspects of American history, which a select few radicals believe or deem offensive, we cancel America's ability or opportunity to learn and know our history. This attitude is very reminiscent of Carl Marx. He wanted to abolish or cancel five things, besides owning private property.

1. The Family

   The family is the basis for the foundation and prosperity for a country.

2. Individuality

   Individuality is a social construct of a capitalist society.

3. Eternal Truths

   Marx did not believe that any truth existed, except for class struggle.

4. Nations

   The working man has no country.

5. Past

The past dominates the present. If you get rid of the past, you can be in control of the future.

The radical left wants to get rid of the family, religion, and eventually the government. They want a free utopian culture and society where everyone can do as they wish. The newer generations are being brainwashed to accept these ideas. Cancel Culture will make it impossible for the more recent generations to understand the background and importance of the past.

The secular world believes that Christians are weak, naive, and unintelligent. Christianity is for fools who need a crutch to lean on. The Church is archaic and narrow-minded. The Church does not allow thinking outside of its dogma. Christianity is judgmental and does not recognize the new *norms* in society today, such as the LGBT movement, multiple genders, and same-sex marriage. Jesus is too personal and interferes in the way they wish to live their lives. Christians are hypocrites, as America has seen many famous pastors sin by having affairs outside of their marriages. Christianity's morals and virtues have been replaced with immediate personal gratification, money, sex, and a post-truth mindset.

The turn away from religion in America is reminiscent of the religious changes in Europe. The beautiful churches in Europe are tourist attractions. Very few people attend religious services in these churches. The Europeans have a culture of many religious wars. Following World War II, Europeans began leaving the Church. Also, European governments started funding the churches, which caused them to be lackadaisical, and they lost their direction. Secularism became the norm in Europe, followed by other countries such as Australia, New Zealand, and Canada. The United States has a different history and culture from Europe. Whereas Europe drifted away from Christianity for the reasons above, the United States is leaving Christianity secondary to the influence of technology, TV, Hollywood, national media, and social media.

Why have I gone through the cultures of the different generations? Understanding the members of the different generations and having an idea about interacting with each generation helps you to know their fundamental beliefs, attitudes, and thought processes. Learning their beliefs and thought processes gives you a better understanding of how best to communicate with them.

Christianity is on the decline in the United States. As Christians, we are called to be disciples of Christ. If you want to be effective in witnessing to others, you need to know how and where to start. The Church needs to change its approach and delivery of God's message. The Church cannot change the message of the grace of Christ, but it needs to change how it reaches out and delivers the Gospel to the young generations. Generation Z or *iGeneration* is the least religious of all the generations! As the Bob Dylan song released in 1964 says in the title, <u>The Times They Are a-Changing</u>. It was true in the 1960s, but is true even more today.

According to Wikipedia, in 1990, 85% of Americans identified themselves as Christian. In 2019, 65% of Americans identified themselves as Christians. Gallop International found that 41% of Americans attend church regularly. Church attendance in other countries is diminishing. For example, regular church attendance in France is only at 15% of the population—United Kingdom 10%—and 7.5% in Australia.

There was a very telling article in the Minneapolis Star Tribune (http://www.startribune.com/as-minnesota-churches-close-a-way-of-life-fades/486037461/) on July 8, 2018, about the failing churches in Minnesota. Since the year 2000, the Evangelical Lutheran Church in America has closed 150 churches. Of the remaining 1,050 Lutheran churches in Minnesota, one-third have fewer members. During the same time, 65 Methodist churches closed.

Scot Thumma, Director of the Hartford Institute for Religion Research (http://hirr.hartsem.edu/), predicts, "In the next twenty years, you will have half as many open congregations as now." One reason is that the people sitting in the pews are getting older— and the younger generations are not attending.

The Southern Baptists have lost more than one million members in the last decade, according to Religion News Service (https://religionnews.com/2018/06/26/why-millennials-are-really-leaving-religion-its-not-just-politics-folks). The speed of decrease will quicken as Generation Z is the most non-Christian generation.

Sometimes surveys have difficulty finding the correct answer, as people do not want to tell the truth about specific topics. The problem of getting correct answers is especially true for people answering questions about religion. The University of Kentucky did a study in 2017 (https://psyarxiv.com/edzda) to get an accurate answer about the prevalence of atheists in America. The problem was that many people do not want to categorize themselves as an atheist. They designed a study asking a series of ten innocuous statements, such as, Do you own a dog? The last statement was, I do not believe in God. The results were that 26% of people answered *yes*. The problem that Christianity is facing may be much larger than realized.

President Dwight Eisenhower signed into law the modern official motto of America, In God We Trust, in 1956. The phrase first appeared on United States coins in 1864. The word *God* is disappearing from our society today. Many secular or liberal people in America have removed the words *under God* from the Pledge of Allegiance. The propaganda from the secular world is changing society and culture in America. Many of the nation's first colleges were founded by Protestant Churches such as Harvard, Yale, Dartmouth, Amherst, Columbia, Duke, Rollins, and Princeton. Most of these schools have removed the emblems of their Protestant heritage.

Members of the Danbury Baptists Association wrote a letter to President-elect Thomas Jefferson in 1801, asking his opinion on a matter. Baptists were in the minority in Connecticut and were required to pay fees to support the Congregationalists who were in the majority. The Baptists were upset that they were forced to support Congregationalists by the Connecticut government. They asked Thomas Jefferson his opinion about religious freedom and the government's support or establishment of religion. President Jefferson wrote back to the Danbury Baptist Association, agreeing that there should be religious freedom from the government. He stated in his letter to them—

Believing with you that religion is a matter which lies solely between man and his God, that he owes account to none other for his faith or his worship, that legislative powers of government reach actions only, and not opinions, I contemplate with sovereign reverence that act of the whole American people which declared that their legislature would "make no law respecting an establishment of religion, or prohibiting the free exercise thereof," thus building a wall of separation between the Church and State.

President Jefferson stated his belief that the Church should be protected from government interference and not what the Supreme Court misinterpreted. President Jefferson was supporting the Church. There was nothing about restricting religion. Instead, it was restricting government interference in religion. The Supreme Court rulings on the separation of Church and State using President's Jefferson's letter to the Baptists were incorrect and taken out of context.

Christianity has been removed from schools, while other religions are allowed in many schools. When I played football in high school, a pastor or priest came into the locker room before each game and said a prayer. The team then said the Lord's Prayer in unison. There was a prayer said over the loudspeaker to everyone attending the game. The band played the National Anthem. Prayer at school events is not allowed any longer. That part of our culture and society has been removed.

The United States is less Christian. The decline in people saying they are Christian is decreasing. The rate of people claiming to be atheist, agnostic, or no beliefs is rising significantly. The secular and spiritual worlds are attacking Christianity on all fronts. They are using flat screens and technology to change our culture and society. The younger generations are having their minds filled with information unrelated to Christianity or anti-Christianity. Unfortunately, children today are raised by flat screens, liberal educators, and peer pressure. Parents have taken a backseat in raising their children. They are living hectic lives and are letting flat screens, schools, and social media raise their children!

Other cultural changes are occurring, which are causing a shift in American society. The gap between the upper class and the lower class is widening. Successful upper class people and the middle class are getting educated and can live in this new world full of technology. But, the lower class people are not educating themselves for a variety of reasons.

Charles Murray wrote a bestselling book in 2012 called Coming Apart. Murray set out to make the case that America is *coming apart* culturally, socially, and economically. The top and bottom of society in America are increasingly living in different cultures. Charles Murray points to several statistics comparing society from 1960 to 2010:

- Marriage was universal, and divorce was rare.
- Out-of-wedlock births rarely happened.
- Illegal drugs were rare.
- It was not socially acceptable for men to be idle and not work.
- Religious values were widely held.

None of these five statements are true today!

Today, we do not want to judge others' actions for anything, even if they are doing something destructive or evil. Having a child outside of wedlock was taboo. Today, over 60 percent of Americans believe it is morally acceptable. The movie Easy Rider in 1969 showed the stars in the movie smoking marijuana—and it was cool. Only 12 percent of Americans supported the legal use of marijuana. Today, the majority of Americans support the legal use of marijuana.

How is this happening? The moral fiber of America is nearly nonexistent. Why do people need so many ways of altering their mental state in order to feel better? People are looking for meaning in life and are ignoring the only true source of peace, hope, joy, and love—Jesus Christ. You will not find the answers about life on social media, a flat screen, in a syringe, or a bottle!

Colossians 2:8 NLT

Don't let anyone capture you with empty philosophies and high-sounding nonsense that come from human thinking and from spiritual powers of this world, rather than from Christ.

You and I live our lives based on our paradigms and worldviews. Understanding your paradigm and worldview is crucial to understanding and living in today's culture and society. Culture and society are not fixed or stationary. Today culture and society are always changing our dynamic, as I said earlier. In the past, generation after generation was the same. Now, each generation is different. What one generation thinks is normal or accepted—another generation thinks it is ridiculous.

Flat screens, social media, politicians, Hollywood, the educational system, and people we look up to influence paradigms and our society. As you will see in a following chapter, everything you see or are exposed to is designed and manipulated to control you. No stone is left unturned to change your thoughts and beliefs.

What you are exposed to is especially crucial for children and young adults. Studies have shown that the amount of time parents spend with their children has decreased by more than 20 hours a week. Parents are letting flat screen and social media train their children's minds. Children need to learn to evaluate everything in this world accurately.

There is a great book that every parent and grandparent should read, written by John Stonestreet and Brett Kunkle. The title is A Practical Guide to Culture and subtitled Helping the Next Generation Navigate Today's World. The book discusses culture and its influence on today's young people. A great thing about the book is that it gives practical step-by-step instructions on communicating and raising children.

Everyone needs to improve their vision, perception, and determination of reality. The Apostle Paul made this point many times in his writings.

Philippians 1:9-10 NLT

I pray that your love will overflow more and more, and that you will keep on growing in knowledge and understanding. For I want you to understand what really matters, so that you may live pure and blameless lives until the day of Christ's return.

The society and culture we live in are essential concerning living a Christian life and spreading the word of Christ's saving grace. T.S. Eliot, an American-British author, is known as one of the most famous poets of any era or generation. But he also wrote a famous book entitled Christianity and Culture. This book provides an exceptional contribution to understanding the nature of culture and Christianity.

He states that a society has ceased to be Christian, when religious practices have been abandoned and behaviors cease to be regulated by reference to Christian principles. Liberalism, the ideology dominant in the West, has emptied out our society (some might say *secularized*), dissolving many of its religiously grounded structures and aims. Culture and religion are so intrinsically intertwined that neither can survive long without the other. The family is the primary channel for the transmission of culture. Culture requires unity. Its people must truly share a way of life. In particular, its people must share a common understanding of their common religious end, in pursuing lives of virtue in this life and beatitude in the next. Without the generation to generation of passing culture, a culture will eventually die. As for the Christian who is not conscious of his dilemma—and he is in the majority— he is becoming more and more de-Christianized by all sorts of unconscious pressure. Paganism holds all the most valuable advertising space.

Is it not intriguing that T.S. Eliot was aware of the media's influence on people's minds before flat screens and social media? Even though there was little media in his time compared to today, he was aware of how visual media can have a brainwashing-like effect on people and society. Culture, family, and God are the backbone of living a good life.

Ethnocentrism is a term coined by William Graham Sumner. It is the tendency to look at the world primarily from the perspective of your ethnicity, culture, and the belief that it is the correct or right way to look at the world. This perspective can lead to incorrect assumptions about others' beliefs and behaviors, based on your norms, beliefs, and values. As an example, the reluctance or unwillingness to try another culture's cuisine is ethnocentric.

Your paradigm, which includes cultural and societal influences, determines your perspective on this world. If you keep locked in your paradigm, your perception of your environment will be skewed. Proper mindset or paradigm development is essential for the younger generations. Their minds have been manipulated to act and believe the way they do. The question is, how can you help your children and grandchildren? The family and the church need to work together. The task of presenting the Gospel of Jesus to younger generations is monumental and utterly different from generations before.

Let us take a little more in-depth look into the Millennials and Generation Z. They are redefining marriage, which is a significant component of culture. They are waiting, on average, until their 30s before getting married. They are skeptical about marriage, as they have seen their parents' divorce and often not in a civil manner. They feel that cohabitation may be a better option than a legally binding marriage. Marriage to them is a legally binding document, religious, and social institution that they do not believe is necessary. How will the family and culture in the future look? How will they relate to religion? A book by Mary Eberstadt called How the West Really Lost God asserts, "The fortunes of religion rise or fall with the state of the family."

What does the average American family look like now? Generations Y and Z are considerably less religious than previous generations. They are less likely to attend any type of church service. Many of these generations have had limited exposure to adult grounded role models who know what they believe, explain why they believe it, and are committed to living by Christian ideals. They do not believe in absolute standards of right or wrong, which I will discuss later. Nearly 25% of them describe their religious beliefs as atheist, agnostic, or nothing at all. Less than one-half of these two generations say religion is important in their lives. They feel that religion is judgmental and everyone has a right to their feelings.

Christianity suffers from an image problem from scandals and affairs. This is primarily due to the liberal press not liking religion and using scandals to denigrate religion. Any negative incident involving the Church is highlighted on TV or social media. The credibility of the Church as a beacon of moral authority has plummeted. Division in the Church regarding abortion, same-sex marriage, gun control, race, and the authority of the Bible has caused much confusion. Christianity is being pushed to the margins of culture and society.

A growing number of people consider Christianity not only foolish, but also immoral due to its alleged intolerance and bigotry. They believe the Church is overprotective and fails to expose people to ideas that may be anti-Christian. The Church's teaching is shallow and narrow-minded. The Church is antagonistic to science and fails to help believers interact with scientific claims. The Church treats sexuality simplistically and judgmentally. The Church makes exclusive claims. The Church is dismissive of doubters. The Church is hypocritical. What makes a Christian any different from me, as we all act the same? For many, the biggest obstacle for Christianity is the actions of other so-called Christians. As talked about in the Great Banquet retreat, you may be the only Bible someone reads.

These generations have been exposed to militant secularism. This secularism has been instilled by the educational system, flat screens, Big Tech, Hollywood, and social media. They have been told that all faith claims are merely expressions of subjective preferences. The only meaningful truth is separated from religion and imposes no moral obligations on human behavior. As seen on TV and social media, the culture in America is a pervasive abandonment of morality in our culture today.

Tolerance is the name of the game, as long as you agree with the far left. Tolerance means that there is no truth or relevant facts—my truth is what counts. No one can question my behavior or beliefs. Anything is allowed and is so ingrained that it is nearly impossible to rationally critique, question, or mention any behavior without the backlash of criticism.

As discussed, the newer generations face different problems than the older generations. The Millennials and Gen Z's have extensive access to information about alternative views. Flat screens, social media, the internet, Hollywood, major news sources, Big Tech, and the government are blasting them with secular information. The Church has failed to provide the Gospel to the younger generations in a manner or form that appeals to them.

Study after study has shown that family is the cornerstone of culture. Young people with a strong family and who have firm religious beliefs use fewer drugs and alcohol, less promiscuity, make better grades in school, and have less depression. The breakdown of the family is especially true in the African American community. A study at the Brookings Institute showed that you could get out of poverty in America by doing three things. If you get a high school diploma, work full-time, and wait until you are 21 to get married and have any children, you will not live in poverty. It is that simple. America is truly the land of freedom, opportunity, and the right to worship God without intervention.

The huge modern heresy is to alter the human soul to fit modern social conditions,   instead of altering modern social conditions to fit the human soul.

— G.K. Chesterton

What are you and I to do about the current situation in society? Hopefully, this book will give insight into recognizing and understanding what is happening in this changing society and culture. We need to teach our children and grandchildren how to use their eyes, develop great perception or discernment, and understand the reality of the information they are watching. Everyone needs to train their ability to analyze the information they are observing.

A drug company representative will come to my office and tell me about a new drug they have developed. The study they show me indicates that it is the best drug. Then go over the research that compares it to their competitor's drug. Their medicine is the best! One hour later, the competitor drug company representative comes to the office and shows me a new study that their drug is the best. They both have a nice graph that reveals their medication is superior. They both cannot be right! If I look at the study's details, there may be a single point in each study that shows they are better. But the final result of the two studies shows they are essentially the same. Both drugs have the same efficacy. You can design a study that gets you the results you want to portray.

During my ophthalmology residency training, we had a journal club meeting each week. Each resident was to review one of the studies in an ophthalmology journal and critique the study. It was surprising how many research studies were done in a poorly designed manner. Therefore, the data or results unsubstantiated.

You need to look carefully, critically, and many times into the information you are observing to know the true answer.

The supreme end of education is expert discernment in all things—the power to tell the good from the bad, the genuine from the counterfeit, and to prefer the good and the genuine to the bad and the counterfeit.

— Samuel Johnson

Fake news never tells the truth. Fake news organizations have an agenda—and they promote that agenda, no matter the actual facts. The fake news, liberal organizations, the educational system, and liberal people talk about being open-minded and caring. But they are intolerant when shown facts opposite of their opinions. They can become hostile and belligerent. Society is exposed to this nonsense. Our young people are being brainwashed to believe that facts and truth are unnecessary. You can make up facts, if needed to support your opinions. We are living in a post-truth society. A great book written by Abdu Murray entitled Saving Truth with the subtitle Finding Meaning and Clarity in a Post-Truth World has terrific information about culture and society today.

It is cool not to be shackled down by truth and facts. You can live a carefree life without any rules and restrictions. Whatever a person feels, whether it is good or right at the moment, is the way to live. What is good or right about something is the opposite of the next day, week, month, or year. This mindset reminds me of the hippie days in the 60s and 70s. These young generations (with the truth does not matter mindset) have difficulty believing the absolute truth of the Gospel. Religion has too many rules and restricts their lifestyle. The Church does not have the same regulations or feelings about their culture, such as views on gender identity, gay lifestyles, sex, and marriage. Some churches have decided not to preach the Gospel, but instead preaches living carefree or a new-age religion. A prosperous and healthy culture cannot maintain itself, if everyone lives by their feelings and continually changes rules. Laws, truth, and facts do not matter. They recognize the facts, but choose to believe their views are what is essential. Their opinions or feelings are what counts.

Radical leftist organizations (such as Black Lives Matter and Antifa) are gaining support from the support of the left-wing media. Internet and social media allows them to reach young people as never before. They are willing to do anything to disrupt this country. These groups are attempting to change society and culture. They certainly have nothing to do with Christianity. They think that life and culture should have no rules or laws. The police need to be defunded. Life should be care-free—and everyone needs to be the same. Many cultures have collapsed from within, such as the Roman Empire, because of social decay. The family and the Church are failing in many respects in America. There is a deepening void between the haves and the have-nots, the educated and the uneducated, and the Christian and the non-Christian.

It is impossible to live a happy and fulfilling life without a set of morals, ethics, truths, or facts on which to live. A culture that believes in God reveals a purpose for living. Parents, grandparents, and the Church need to develop communication methods that will appeal to these generations. You and I need to educate ourselves. These two books are a great start.

- A practical Guide to Culture/ Helping the Next Generation Navigate Today's World by John Stonestreet and Brett Kunkle

- Saving Truth / Finding Meaning and Clarity in a Post-Truth World by Abdu Murray

The mindset of the Millennials and Gen Z is dramatically different from the previous generations. Parents and grandparents need to arm themselves with information on how to communicate with their young loved ones. Discussing important matters with them can be stressful. As you know, they do not believe in absolute truths or, in many instances, even simple facts. If you come on too strong with them, you will be rejected. You need to have calm and loving communication with them. Through the example of your life, be a light to light their pathway through this treacherous world of today.

The Judeo-Christian foundation of culture, society, and the Government in America is rapidly vanishing. It is being replaced with anarchy. All generations are being affected by the overload of information blasting our eyeballs! Society is falling apart (secondary to its stresses) through flat screens, job demands, destruction of the family unit, worry, fear, and anxiety. Many people have exceeded their limits of handling stress and mental disease has become widespread.

There is a book by Richard A. Swenson M.D. entitled Margin: How to Create the Emotional, Physical, Financial, and Time Reserves You Need. Dr. Swenson believes that all this technology has benefited us in many ways. It also brings pains and problems that must be ruthlessly resisted, if life, society, and culture are to be balanced—especially Christian living.

Margin is *the space that once existed between ourselves and our limits*. When you reach the limits of your resources and abilities, you are out of margin. As discussed earlier, your brain is processing five times more information than people a generation or two ago. This staggering amount and content of information are pushing society to its limits. You and I may not have the stress of discovering the West in a covered wagon, or wondering if our crops will make it this planting season, but we face many other things. Traffic congestion, terrorism, litigious society, divorce rate, drugs, alcoholism, the prevalence of sexual diseases, confusion of sexual orientation, road rage, 24-hour news cycles that fixate on the negative or sensational events, money, health, and bullying are just a few of the stresses in life today. On top of all those stress-inducing things, people are overstimulating the emotional area or limbic system, with extreme things they are addicted to on their flat screens. No wonder alcoholism and drug addiction are so prevalent! The number of deaths from drug overdose and car accidents by drunk drivers has skyrocketed!

People are reaching their limits and are suffering because of the stress and anxiety in today's world. As discussed in Chapter 5, people need to think about taking a Dopamine Fast. Turn off the flat screen! Spend time with God and the Bible, yourself, and family! Develop some safety in your margins of life. Don't burn the candle at both ends, get adequate sleep, and exercise.

Culture and society are part of everyone's life. Culture, society, the family, and Christianity need to be intertwined to prosper and survive the attacks. A prospering and vibrant society cannot survive unless Christianity, the family, and the country's cultures are intimately connected. Culture and society are constantly and rapidly changing because of technology.

It is in Christianity that our arts have developed; it is in Christianity that the laws of Europe- until recently- have been rooted. It is against a background of Christianity that all our thought has significance. An individual European may not believe that the Christian faith is true, and yet what he says, and makes, and does will all spring out of his heritage of Christian culture and depend upon that culture for its meaning... I do not believe that the culture of Europe could survive the complete disappearance of the Christian faith. And I am convinced of that, not merely because I am a Christian myself, but as a student of social biology. If Christianity goes, the whole culture goes.

— T.S. Eliot

Understanding and knowing about the cultures of today will improve your ability to communicate, advise, and nurture your loved ones. The knowledge about culture and society will improve your ability to see, perceive, and realize reality. It will help you interact with others. If you are a Christian and a disciple of Christ, you are a witness to the world. You, and I, and the Church need to improve the way we witness to the world, especially to the younger generations. Everyone needs to have the opportunity to grow up in a healthy family unit, get a good education, and be told about the amazing grace of Jesus Christ. Everyone needs to communicate and behave lovingly and kindly.

Colossians 4:5-6 NLT

Live wisely among those who are not believers and make the most of every opportunity. Let your conversation be gracious and attractive so that you will have the right response for everyone.

Chapter 7

The Power of Visual Communication

and

How the Secular World Tries to Change Your Perception

If you tell a lie long enough, it will become the truth.

The statement above has been attributed to Adolf Hitler and his propaganda chief, Joseph Goebbels. There is evidence that it existed before them, but most people consider that these two extensively promoted it first. There are other terms for this—the illusion of truth, truth effect, validity effect, reiteration effect, and illusory truth effect. These terms relate to the tendency to believe that false statements or information are correct after repeated exposure. Another similar statement is: Want to make a lie seem true? Say it again. And again. And again.

This rarely discussed phenomenon of repetition, or the Illusory Truth Effect, was first studied in 1977 at Villanova University and Temple University. The study was titled, <u>Frequency and the Conference of Referential Validity</u>. When the truth is assessed, people depend on whether the statement or information aligns

119

with their beliefs or if they feel it is familiar information. The first conclusion is logical, as people compare new statements with what they know as true. The second conclusion relies on the statement being familiar; therefore if you have heard it many times before, it is true. Your brain is an excellent pattern-matcher and rewards us for using this helpful skill. Repetition creates a pattern (which naturally the brain picks up first) and then creates the comfort of familiarity. Repetition makes a lie appear true.

Familiarity can overpower rationality or what you know as true—and repetitively hearing a false statement can alter a person's beliefs! A study in the Journal of Experimental Psychology by Lisa K. Fazio, Nadia M. Brasier, Keith Payne, and Elizabeth J. Marsh titled, "Knowledge Does Not Protect Against Illusory Truth" showed that the truth-effect could influence participants who knew the correct answer in the beginning, but who were swayed to believe otherwise through the repetition of a false statement. The illusion of truth-effect works just as powerfully for known facts, as well as unknown facts—suggesting that prior knowledge will not prevent repetition from swaying your judgment of plausibility. Repetition has the power to make things sound more valid, even when you know differently!

The power of repetition has been known for centuries, but only scientifically proven recently. Roman statesman Cato closed each of his speeches with a call to destroy Carthage—knowing the repetition would cause agreement among the people. Napoleon reportedly said, "There is only one figure in the rhetoric of serious importance, namely, repetition." As I said earlier, Hitler and Stalin used repetition to their advantage.

Today, repetition is used by election campaigns, advertising, news media, political propaganda, the internet, and social media. The liberal news media know this very well and works together to influence everyone. When a story breaks, they all say the exact same phrase to describe their point of view. Even though they are competitors in the news business, the different news outlets agree to work together to push a secular liberal agenda. The power of persuasion to influence the public overrides their competitiveness. You see the same phrase or information repeatedly by all the mass news media. Therefore, they can make any statement, no matter how outrageous, true!

Adolf Hitler coined the Big Lie propaganda technique. Is it not interesting that the liberal media uses Nazi techniques to persuade you? Hitler talked about utilizing a lie so colossal that no one would believe that someone could have the impudence to distort the truth so infamously. His primary rules were: never allow the public to cool off—never admit a fault or wrong—never concede that there may be some good in your enemy—never leave room for alternatives—never accept blame—concentrate on one enemy at a time and blame them for everything that goes wrong—people will believe a big lie sooner than a little one—and, if you repeat it enough, people will sooner or later believe it.

How about this example of a colossal lie! While I am writing this book, riots are occurring across America in cities run by liberal mayors and liberal governors. These liberal governments are allowing the rioting to continue unabated. According to them, it is a summer of love and peace. The schizophrenic news media shows a reporter on a street where the riots are happening. He states, "It is a march or protest which is peaceful and quiet. These people there are just expressing their first amendment rights." The scene behind him is chaos. Buildings are burning, people are screaming, and thugs destroying private property and looting businesses. You would think that 100% of the people watching the broadcast would be appalled by what they saw behind him. There would be no way that anyone would believe the rioters are peaceful!

How brazen they have become, as they can tell you the protests are quiet and peaceful while showing you a video of chaos, looting, and burning buildings. But they are very confident in their abilities. They know if they tell you they are peaceful enough times, you will believe them. The truth does not matter! Their plan of radical left-wing philosophy is more important.

You might be thinking, I am too smart to fall for that kind of tactic. More intelligent people are not susceptible to having their beliefs changed that way, right? Sorry to say, but wrong! Research has shown that the people with the most education, highest mathematical skills, strongest tendencies, and confident about their beliefs are more likely to resist true information about an issue that is different from their beliefs. They justify what they already believe and are sure they are correct. They find reasons to dismiss any new true facts.

If you have been indoctrinated into false beliefs through America's liberal education system, you believe in their false narrative. People keep repeating false statements, because they are unable to analyze any new information correctly. Their closed minds or paradigms embed the belief deeper and deeper into their brains. In most cases, you are making a mistake to think that you can change or correct a person's view on an issue by giving them more facts.

The secular activist liberal world will use any and all methods to persuade you to believe in their way of life. The propaganda they use is a deliberate, systematic process to shape perceptions and beliefs, manipulate cognitions, and change behaviors to achieve their goal of changing culture and society. They use propaganda to invoke an emotional response to their cause. Propaganda is endowed with negative connotative meanings in today's society. The secular world uses false facts, partial truths, statements out of context, selective information, and transmits only those ideas needed to accomplish their goals.

America was founded on a Judeo-Christian religious basis. One of the secular world's main focuses is to get rid of Christianity, so that a socialist or totalitarian system can emerge. Propaganda is found everywhere today, as technology and flat screens flood you with information all day long. Propaganda is found in national news organizations, advertising, journalism, the educational system, public relations, social media, and nearly all aspects of your daily life.

Public relations professionals specialize in communication and provide their clients with the techniques needed to promote their message to you. There are four public relations specialists for every journalist. Society is turning into an activist liberal society, trying to create social change. Activists and, in many cases, terrorist groups, such as Antifa and Black Lives Matter, are trying to tear apart the fabric of American life. Through public relations with the national news media and Big Tech's support, they try to make people believe they are good people, just trying to make America a better nation. They are trying to change America and its Judeo-Christian heritage radically.

Propaganda uses all forms of visual communication to spread its message. Propaganda can be so powerful that everyone can be susceptible to it. There is way too much information entering your brain, making it impossible to process all the data. Anyone trying to influence you knows that your mind will change, if they blast you with enough information. YouTube and Twitter were essential tools that ISIS used to recruit people to their cause. Many of the people recruited had no knowledge or belief system related to ISIS, but they were radicalized into terrorists from social media propaganda.

This use of social media is known as the Dune Affect. The Dune Affect was coined after the book and movie <u>Dune</u>, written by Frank Herbert in 1965. It is considered one of the best science-fiction books of all time. In <u>Dune</u>, the underlying premise was that whoever controlled the spice and the communications channels controlled the universe. In the book, Spice extends human life, provides superhuman levels of thought, and makes faster-than-light travel possible. It is the most valuable commodity in the universe. The Dune Affect is based on the belief that whoever controls and has access to media, has access to and potential control of public opinion. Jim Morrison of the band, The Doors, said, "Whoever controls the media, controls the mind."

Truth is so obscure in these times, and falsehood so established, that, unless we love the truth, we cannot know it

— Blaise Pascal 17th Century

How are you to combat all this propaganda, false information, and mind-changing information you are observing? What is real and what is true? One method to combat the repetition of propaganda is to always have curiosity and an open mind about what you are observing. Do not let a closed mind blind you from seeing what is true. Change the way you look at things, and the things you look at, change. The national news media, organizations, social media, Big Tech, and advertisers study everyone's actions and responses to what they see. They form focus groups and develop studies to know how the average American reacts to everything they present to you. They are willing to lie or say anything, if it will influence you.

Colossians 2:8 NLT

Don't let anyone capture you with empty philosophies and high-sounding nonsense that comes from human thinking and from the spiritual powers of this world, rather than from Christ

The truth can sometimes be challenging to find. The major news organizations began telling everyone things that I did not believe to be true many years ago. Then in 2001, Bernard Goldberg let out the truth about his fellow journalists and news organizations. He wrote a book called <u>Bias: A CBS Insider Exposes How the Media Distort the News</u>. Goldberg won 14 Emmy Awards and was a producer, reporter, and correspondent for CBS News for 28 years. He could no longer sit by and watch CBS distort or slant the news to fit the agenda they wanted to support—a liberal and secular bias. Of course, CBS immediately fired Goldberg, as he had let the cat out of the bag. A producer at MSNBC, Adriana Pekary, quit her job in July of 2020, because she could longer be a part of the news MSNBC produced.

Flat screens, social media, news media, the internet, and Big Tech change the way you live your life—and they shape the way you believe, whether you recognize that it is happening or not. The practice of intentionally guiding or changing user behavior is known as *persuasive technology*. Stanford researcher B.J. Fogg is the father of persuasive technology. He referred to this field of study as *captology* or CAPT in 1996. CAPT or captology comes from Computers as Persuasive Technologies. Captology is the study of how every aspect of computer productions viewed on flat screens (such as computers, smartphones, websites, apps, and video games) are used to change attitudes or behaviors.

Another term for technology influencing culture and society is called *Technology Determinism*. Technology Determinism explains the ways technology determines the structure and values of a society. Technology exerts societal influence, creates an environment, and even determines human behaviors. As technology advances and their influences are incorporated into society, it will immediately alter activities and behaviors. These changes also have a ripple effect or long-term effect that defines culture and society. This effect also alters religious beliefs and practices.

Can technology companies and developers design persuasive systems that can be used and monetized? Yes! They are continually developing new products and methods to influence you. The developers follow three criteria developed by Fogg's Theory of behavior change. Three criteria must be fulfilled for you to do what they want you to do.

You must want to do it.

You must be able to do it.

You must be promoted to do it.

They are effective only when you are highly motivated to do it or when the task is easy. Persuasive technology is used in social media feeds—Amazon one-click checkout, fingerprint log on to your smartphone, apps, weight-loss apps helping you with your diet, and a large number of others.

An example is Netflix. Netflix designed its system that automatically plays the next episode of a show you are watching, unless you click the remote to stop it. They end the current episode of a movie series with a scene that makes you want to see the next episode. You are motivated to continue watching the next episode and the next episode. You end up binge-watching a series. It takes more effort to stop playing the show, than letting it begin the next episode. The next episode starts automatically. Netflix designed its system to persuade the viewer to keep watching and using its services.

Netflix and other companies make it easier to continue a subscription than to cancel it. Captology is everywhere, and those who understand capitalize on it. In the realm of persuasive technology, people are not aware that they are being persuaded!

Smartphones persuade you to repeatedly check your phone when you hear the signal for a new message, causing a dopamine release. You look at your smartphone more than one hundred times a day! Psychologists have identified that instant messaging and texting are addictive. The dopamine release addicts you to your phone.

Mass media communication, communication theory, media influence, and media effects are topics related to the media's effects on society, culture, and changing people's attitudes, thoughts, beliefs, and behaviors. Mass media influences nearly everything you do or believe. The media tries to influence your vote, views, knowledge, beliefs, opinions, and actions. They skew or lie about the information they are supplying.

I no longer watch any major news broadcasts, because I know the lies they will tell before they say it. I get my news from research and sources that I believe are telling the truth. The media is now totally leftist and will say anything to support their view. The way the media selects, takes things out of context, shapes and molds its presentation is designed for one purpose—press their liberal secular agenda.

Every aspect of how you react to the information you watch or observe has been studied and is continually reviewed. The human brain works similarly in everyone. The vast majority of people will succumb to the influence of basic psychological tricks. There are studies after studies on people's reactions to various stimuli. These people are not kidding around. There are billions and trillions of dollars at stake—presidential campaigns, power, control of society, and culture.

The media, corporations, government, news organizations, marketing companies, political campaigns, left-wing organizations, Big Tech, and many others use these proven ways to influence you.

Agenda-Setting Theory describes how topic selection and frequency of reporting effects and influences public opinion.

Framing identifies how the media tries to manipulate the people's opinions through control of camera angles, lighting, magnification of the image, facts, opinions, and the amount of coverage applied to a topic.

Cultivation Theory tries to change perceptions over time through continuous exposure. You grow to like and trust the national news commentator over time.

The Decoy Effect causes you to perform a particular action, such as buying the product they want you to buy. A classic example is the movie theater. The theater wants you to buy the most expensive box of popcorn. The small box of popcorn costs $3.00, and the large box of popcorn costs $7.00. When given only these two choices, almost no one ever buys the large $7.00 box. But if they put in the decoy offer of a medium box of popcorn for $6.50, many people will buy the large box, because it is only 50 cents more but much larger. The medium popcorn is the decoy to get you to buy the large box at $7.00.

Scarcity Theory is the principle that goes back to the supply and demand formula. The rarer the product or commodity, the more valuable it is. You might remember a Travelocity Travel website commercial about several men checking into a hotel. They were talking about the great price each got for their room. Each man got a different price from different websites and was told there were only two rooms left at that low price—and then the prices were going up. Each man paid a different price—and each man was bragging that he got the best price. The men were enticed to purchase the room as a travel website told them there were only two rooms left at that price. They were also enticed to purchase a room for the current price on the website because of the fear of the price going up. It turns out that that information was not correct. The commercial was about Travelocity. The man who purchased his room the day before on Travelocity had a better price than everyone else. The price had not gone up.

Loss Aversion Theory is that most people would rather avoid a loss than gain something. The pain a person feels from a loss is two times as strong as a reward from a gain. A $20 voucher is not as good as $20 off your next purchase.

Anchoring Theory is used to entice you to purchase an item. The store states the initial price or anchor and displays the sales price right next to the original price. The sales price is always in red, because the color red promotes action.

These are just a few of the techniques used to influence you. All day, every day, you are exposed to these types of techniques.

In the chapter on flat screens, I told you about how much time everyone is spending on different devices. Let us go over some information about what you are exposed to while watching flat screens that are changing culture and society. Flat screen time is especially important for younger people with brains that are still developing.

Over 60% of Americans watch TV while they are eating dinner. So much for family time at the dinner table. A new study revealed that the average parent spends only four minutes a week of meaningful conversation with their children. Americans spend 250 billion hours a year watching TV. A child watches TV for over 1,500 minutes a week. By the time a child finishes elementary school, they have watched 8,000 murders. On graduation from high school, a young person has witnessed 200,000 acts of violence. The average American is watching programs with little input of valuable information. Americans can name The Three Stooges 60% of the time, while 17% can't name three U.S. Supreme Court justices. You have seen two million TV commercials by age 65.

Every morning nearly everyone's first instinct is to reach for their smartphone or turn on the TV. You wake up scrolling through emails, notifications, tweets, Pinterest, Facebook, Snapchat, and others.

Maybe you wake up and immediately start playing a video game. I have a friend and ophthalmology colleague who became addicted to video games. The video game business is a multi-billion-dollar business that creates games that stimulates the mind and is very addictive. The games are designed to cause a release of dopamine in the brain. Doctor Andrew Doan and Brooke Strickland wrote a book about video game addiction. Doctor Doan is a well-respected ophthalmologist, but he became addicted to video games and the thrill of them. He spent over 20,000 hours playing games. Doctor Doan's reckless compulsion to play games transformed him into a monster that almost destroyed his family, marriage, and career. The book he wrote is titled <u>Hooked on Games: The Lure and Cost of Video Game and Internet Addiction</u>. He shares his expertise to educate others on the dangers of video addiction and provide hope for video addicts and their families.

Social media has many positive benefits, but it has also robbed people of individual attributes. It has taken away from many people the ability to find trust and comfort with one another. We have replaced this personal interaction with a hollow virtual relationship with others. The younger generations have limited social and physical interactions with their peers. According to a journal article by Jacob Amedie titled, <u>The Impact of Social Media on Society</u>, *Each step forward in social media has made it easier, just a little, to avoid the emotional work of being present, to convey information rather than humanity.* Amedie also states, that social media *robs us of self-control and from the ability to think independently and instead makes us gullible to join any group that posts perverse messages that tickle our ears and amuse our senses without evaluation the consequences.*

Many experts in social media believe there are short-term and long-term effects secondary to social media use. The short-term effects are priming, arousal, and mimicry. A lot of this is from the dopamine released into the brain from the stimulation of social media. Priming processes occur in the brain by being excited from participating in social media. There is increased arousal, secondary to stimulation from social media. Mimicry occurs from the time spent viewing social media. You tend to mimic or copycat what is on social media.

The long-term effects are more chronic and lasting, such as observational learning of thoughts and behaviors, activation and desensitization of emotional centers in the limbic system. Observational learning is especially true in the developing brains of children. They are molding and developing their paradigm or beliefs. Desensitization occurs after repeated exposure to emotionally stimulating social media or video games. Continued viewing can lead to the habituation of emotional responses to visual stimuli.

God made you and me social beings. You need the companionship of other human beings to live a happy, successful life. The strength of your interactions with others has a significant impact on your mental health as well. Having friends helps relieve anxiety, provides comfort, decreases stress, prevents loneliness, prevents depression, and extends your life expectancy. In the virtual world of social media, you do not have real-world interactions with other people.

Many studies have shown a strong connection between extended social media use and an increased risk of anxiety, loneliness, and depression. Many people use social media as a security blanket. They go on social media when stressed, instead of talking or meeting with a friend in person. Social media can cause a horrible cycle of an unhealthy addiction from spending long periods on it. The suicide rate in the age group of 10 to 24 has increased by approximately 60 percent from 2007—2018. The numbers in the year 2020 increased significantly. The isolation from the pandemic has caused significant mental stress. Nearly 75 percent of people aged 18-24 in the year 2020 have reported at least one adverse cognitive or behavioral health symptom. The leading causes of death in young people are 1. Accidents 2. Suicide 3. Homicide. How sad is it that the second and third leading cause of death for our young people in the United States is suicide and homicide? You would have trouble decreasing the accident rate, but suicide and homicide are preventable.

Social media has a significant impact on interpersonal communication and relationships, job interviews, and employment. What you see or post will follow you wherever you go. People are losing their college scholarships and jobs because of their activity on social media. Approximately sixty percent of employers use social networking sites to research job candidates.

The social media landscape is changing constantly and rapidly. Social media is a massive part of people's lives, like it or not. Social media is not a true or real world. At the present rate of people's use today, you will spend nearly seven years of your life on social media. Social media is a human marketplace. It is a virtual place that is shiny and bright. It is where you post the prettiest and best pictures to tell everyone about your best news. People or companies try to convince you how great their life is— and yours is not as good. You need their product—or if it is an individual, it makes social media a fairyland where everything about them is perfect. There is a danger of slipping too far into that virtual world, losing your sense of real facts, real life, real self, and true reality. If you perceive that everyone else on social media is perfect, you can push yourself into becoming someone you are not and become frustrated and depressed.

Big Tech wants to further its influence over the world with their next initiative, expanding social media with the *metaverse*. This term was coined by Neal Stephenson in his science fiction novel Snow Crash, where humans as avatars interact with each other in a 3D virtual space. The term is a combination of the prefix "meta," meaning beyond and the universe. This is a virtual reality-based successor to the internet. This technology will entice people to spend all their time in a virtual reality world with adventures, games, shopping, and unlimited potential to dream up entertainment scenarios.

The metaverse is a massive communal cyberspace linking virtual reality and augmented reality together, enabling avatars to jump instantly from one scenario to another activity. This is similar to a technology being developed by Nissan called invisible to visible. Nissan is going to overlay the car's windshield with virtual information, as well as the ability to summon an in-car 3D avatar. Big Tech is going to keep expanding technology to control everyone. They will have you addicted and blind to the ultimate reality of life!

Nearly 70% of people get their news from social media. Most mass-media campaigns have the central mission of changing your perception of reality. The reality they are promoting may pertain to a political campaign, selling a product, promoting a cause, or changing the culture and society. You may not be able to discern the reality or purpose of the communication, because of your present paradigm or beliefs. You are systematically exposed to images that are not representing reality, but propose that they are true. The cognitive processing of information presented to you repeatedly causes the brain to believe that it is true. You may believe you have an optimistic bias and feel less vulnerable than others to the media information onslaught and propaganda. But do you?

The mass media, game developers, marketing firms, corporations, the government, app developers, Big Tech, and others spend large amounts of money and time studying your responses to the things you observe and watch. They want to control you and your thought processes, beliefs, and actions. So, why are they doing this? Corporations and businesses want you to purchase their products. For others, the motive is not so obvious. These groups wish to control everything in your life. The people running the government want to be in charge, because you are incapable of making the right decisions about your life. They want the power to be in control and the wealth that goes with it. They push a socialized society, a communist way of living, or totalitarian rule of all life's aspects.

Who is trying to change culture and society? The radical left-wing people and organizations (Antifa and Black Lives Matter), left-wing ideologues of the government, Big Tech, major news organizations, and businesses with radical leftist beliefs and totalitarian agendas are trying to change America. The power of visual communication is under the control of very few groups or individuals. Microsoft (Bill Gates), Apple (originally Steve Jobs), Facebook (Mark Zuckerberg), Amazon (Jeff Bezos), Google (Larry Page and Sergey Bren), and Twitter (Jack Dorsey) control the narrative. They are other sources such as Instagram and WhatsApp, owned by Facebook. Google owns YouTube. The other players are the news outlets and the government. These people control nearly everything you see or watch. You are slowly and insidiously becoming habituated to sharing your data all the time. You get accustomed to Big Tech and the Government monitoring and tracking you.

The United States is becoming a totalitarian state. I have talked with people who fled Cuba and the Eastern Block of countries. They believe that it is happening here today. You are being offered everything for free, even if you are not a citizen of the United States. There is free college tuition, healthcare, housing, free telephones, and many other free gifts or rights. A totalitarian regime means no religion. Religious freedoms are being taken away, such as no prayer in school and the wrong interpretation of church and state separation. States run by these radical leftist governments stopped church services during the Corona 19 pandemic. It is perfectly acceptable to riot, burn down buildings, and loot businesses, but you cannot go to church! They are breaking the laws of the Constitution, but could care less. Their cause is more important. Unfortunately, the United States Attorney General and The United States Supreme Court are unwilling to stop it.

Totalitarianism is the concept of a government or political system that prohibits opposition, restricts individuals, and controls people's public and private lives. It is the most extreme form of authoritarianism. The government is characterized by a lack of democracy, total control over the economy, censorship, limited freedom of movement, mass surveillance, religious persecution, state atheism, and widespread cultism. In the more severe cases—concentration camps, secret police, and executions.

I do not think we are headed to a totalitarian state like Adolf Hitler (former head of Nazi Germany), Joseph Stalin (former head of the Communist Party of the Soviet Union), Benito Mussolini (former Duce of Italy), or Nicolas Maduro (President of Venezuela). But we are heading towards Digital Totalitarianism or Soft Totalitarianism. George Orwell used the term *totalitarian* in many essays that he published from 1940 to 1942. He feared that future totalitarian regimes would exploit technology in mass media and surveillance, to establish a worldwide dictatorship that would be incapable of ever being overthrown.

Digital Totalitarianism is already here in many aspects. Remember Edward Snowden, who blew the whistle about government surveillance and fled to Russia. The former United States systems analyst denounced the government's efforts to monopolize and militarize innovations in the field of telecommunications—taking advantage of the natural human desire to communicate and exploit it to obtain unlimited power.

"It's through the use of new platforms and algorithms that are built on and around these capabilities that they are able to shift our behavior. In some cases, they are able to predict our decisions and also nudge them to different outcomes," Snowden said. He argued that modern militarized technology, with the help of social media and corporate giants, is allowing governments to become **the almighty** given the magnitude of their ability to monitor, analyze, and influence behavior of people. Snowden believes that the human desire to feel part of a social group is being exploited, as internet users consent to provide their personal data, signing written agreements that they rarely read. It sounds like we are already into Digital Totalitarianism in the United States today.

Many of the business apps you are using track your location and send you advertisements when you are near their store. The app will ask you if they can monitor your location at all times or only when using the app. Many people say OK to the app following them. But, if you only allow them to locate you when using the app, do they really leave you alone? I can hire a tech company to send messages or send you to my website when you are near any eye care facility—to try to block you from that eye center and instead see my information. Of course, I am the best ophthalmologist in The United States, and you need to see me, right? (My propaganda!!)

Employers are using technology to track and monitor their employees. UPS places sensors in its trucks to track the truck's location, speed of the truck, monitoring the opening and closing doors of the truck, and clicking of seat belts. Amazon is looking into an electronic wristband that would be used to monitor hand movements, to monitor how much work their employees are doing. Software developed at Stanford University enables anyone to manipulate video footage in real time. So now, you do not know if what you are seeing is the truth, or you are seeing what someone wants you to see!

China has already developed into a digital or surveillance totalitarian state. They are following their citizens and dictate what the people of China can say, post, or do through their smartphones. China uses special algorithms for consumer data, GPS tracking, facial responses, and other forms of surveillance to monitor its citizens. If they are found doing anything the State deems inappropriate, there will be ramifications, such as reducing their credit on their smartphones. They pay for everything through their phones, so that everything is monitored.

Maybe there will not be a 666 tattooed on everyone, but everyone will be required to live their lives connected to a smartphone. Look out if there is a model number 666! In a digital totalitarian society, the State or Big Brother, or Big Tech may have the power to control your bank account and shut off access to the bank if they decide to do so.

Facebook has hired several nationals from China who are experts in "Hate Speech Engineering" or what they really mean is *censorship*. The Chinese are experts in censorship algorithms. Facebook and Twitter recently blocked the New York Post report about Hunter Biden's laptop. They blocked the New York Post, anyone trying to comment on the story, and stopped it from becoming a huge national story. Typically, the major news organizations would not be too happy about Big Tech censoring them. But since they agreed with the cause behind the censorship, nearly all the other major news media outlets supported Facebook and Twitter. Who are they going to censor next?

You and I have been extensively studied as to our viewing habits and reactions to what we watch. People have spent millions of dollars researching how to use propaganda to support their agenda. Propaganda manipulates the mind, to bring about changes in thought processes and eventually to change the family, religion, and society. Propaganda is a unique form of communication studied in communication research. Media impact research focuses on media manipulation. Propaganda campaigns follow a strategic set of parameters, techniques, and strategies to indoctrinate the public. These techniques are categorized through psychological analysis within mass psychology, social psychology, political psychology, and cognitive psychology with cognitive distortions.

The propaganda basics create intense emotions, simplify the information, appeal to people's needs and values, and attack the opposition.

There are seventy or more specific techniques identified used in persuasion and propaganda. Here is a list of a few of them: appeal to authority, appeal to fear, appeal to prejudice, classical conditioning, demonizing of the enemy, disinformation, false accusations, half-truths, information overload, labeling, lying, deception, and operant conditioning to name a few. You and I have been gone over by a fine-toothed comb. They will continue to study people's responses to improve their ability to influence the masses.

These individuals and organizations are spreading propaganda everywhere there is a flat screen. Every single image or video you see is trying to influence you. Often, this may be benign, such as trying to sell you a car; and of course, theirs is the best; or they may brainwash you to believe their agenda. Unfortunately, the mind is susceptible to the bombardment of their message. All the images that enter your brain are processed, most of which are sent to your subconscious. The images you see in the media are never randomly chosen. A picture of someone they support will be smiling, and the image of someone they do not support will be scowling or frowning. In all the images you see in advertising, the people are happy, attractive, sexier, carefree, and successful. You need their product. Propaganda is primal. All advertising appeals to your deepest emotions.

What is all this propaganda and brainwashing doing to culture and society? Why are the Millennials and Generation Z (Zoomers) young people leaving Christianity? Flat screens and technology are directing the younger generations away from God. Most of them believe that Christianity is judgmental and anti-gay. These generations lack authentic spiritual role models to follow, as they live in broken families. They spend most of their lives on a flat screen and diminished time with family togetherness. There are many books, blogs, and social media outlets promoting atheism. Atheism is a new popular subject on the internet. Buddhism and Islam are just one click away. These generations believe my truth is my truth, and you cannot question my beliefs or behavior.

The trend towards decreasing religion is probably here to stay, unless the family and the Church make a comeback. One of the most significant factors in developing religious affiliation is being raised in a Christian home. A smaller portion of the last several generations has a stable family and a religious upbringing. Religion is diminishing with each generation.

Many Christians, especially the younger generations, are turning to apps for their faith, instead of churches. What will the future of churches look like in the future, if they are unable to appeal to the younger generations? The Church is going to need to change its presentation of the Gospel.

There is an interesting story about Reverend Pete Phillips. He moved to Durham several years ago. He is the Codec Research Center director at Durham University in the United Kingdom. He was ejected from the city's cathedral, because he was reading the Bible on his smartphone. Phones were not allowed in the holy place and he was asked to leave. The Durham Cathedral is 1,000 years old, but its phone policy was not current with today's times. They have now changed their policy.

The digital age is going to change Christianity in other ways, as well. Reading Scripture on an iPad or smartphone can influence how the Scripture is interpreted. Reading bite-sized nuggets of the Bible changes how the Bible is read. Studies have shown that text read on flat screens is generally taken more literally than text read in books. You tend to comprehend broader themes and emotional content when you read Scriptures in a book. When you read on a flat screen, you tend to miss out on the Scripture's emotional aspect and read it factually. It is like nonemotionally flat reading, rather than the feeling of reading a sacred text. A new kind of religion is appearing from the use of technology. Millennials prefer a more distant generalized picture of God. They prefer God to Jesus. Jesus is too personal and might interfere with their personal lives.

In comparison, God is up in heaven and more non-specific. With technology, it is easier to develop an individualized faith or religion. You and I have more access to all kinds of information, viewpoints, and we can personalize our beliefs. You can watch a flat screen for your church service, but you lose the fellowship of personal interaction with other Christians. You can become isolated, just like the Millennials and Zoomers, with the resulting problems that have been discussed previously.

In the year 2020, the isolation from quarantine due to Covid-19 has caused all kinds of mental and physical health problems. Humankind was not made to live in isolation. During this pandemic, the mind becomes more accepting of the power of visual communication. Everyone has spent the year watching more flat screens due to the quarantine.

There has been an increase in Totalitarianism in America in the last several years, which is especially true for 2020 and 2021. The Totalitarianism of today is dramatically different from Nazi Germany and Stalin's Russia. Their totalitarian regimes were draconian or brutal. They gained power by killing millions of people and putting anyone who opposed them to death or in concentration camps or gulags. This new Totalitarianism is different from the hard and harsh regimes previously. Rod Dreher, in his book, describes it as Soft Totalitarianism. The book is titled Live Not by Lies, with the subtitle A Manual for Christian Dissidents. It is a great read. Sheldon Wolin coined another term called *Inverted Totalitarianism*. I like the *term Incognito Totalitarianism* as this new form of Totalitarianism is camouflaged and deceptive. Most people are unaware that society is being changed to a totalitarian system.

Alexis de Tocqueville is a famous French aristocrat, diplomat, political scientist, and historian who visited the United States in 1831. He wrote several books and articles about what he observed on his visit. He was most famous for his book titled Democracy in America. Here are a couple of his famous quotes.

Society is endangered not by the great profligacy of a few, but by the laxity of morals amongst all.

It's not an endlessly expanding list of rights – the 'right' to education, the 'right' to healthcare, the 'right' to food and housing. That's not freedom, that's dependency. Those aren't rights, those are the rations of slavery –hay and a barn for human cattle.

Democracy extends the sphere of individual freedom, socialism restricts it. Democracy attaches all possible value to each man; socialism makes each man a mere agent, a mere number. Democracy and socialism have nothing in common but one word: equality. But notice the difference: while democracy seeks equality in liberty, socialism seeks equality in restraint and servitude.

Having thus taken each citizen in turn in its powerful embrace and shaped him to its will, government then extends its embrace to include the whole society. It covers the whole of social life with a network of petty, complicated rules that are both minute and uniform... It does not break men's will, but softens, bends, and guides it; it seldom enjoins, but often inhibits actions; it does not destroy anything, but prevents much being born; it is not at all tyrannical, but it hinders, restrains, enervates, stifles, and stultifies so much that in the end each nation is no more than a flock of timid and hardworking animals with the government as its shepherd.

— Alexis Tocqueville

Do his words describe America today? It is hard to read these words without wincing. Tocqueville believes the result is that America would turn to a despotic government, featuring officials who rule more like schoolmasters than tyrants. I think the United

States has moved beyond Tocqueville's soft despotism to a new and more dangerous social control form. Conservative speakers are banned from college campuses. Facebook and Twitter block or ban many conservatives and religious opinions. Liberal content is allowed, even when it is abusive and vulgar. Big Tech controls nearly all the visual content you watch and cancel anything they do not like!

The family and religion used to be the bedrock of society. They are systematically and surreptitiously being destroyed. The success of these institutions is gradually being diminished. You may be fired from your work for your religious beliefs or expelled from school for your Christian faith.

Sheldon Wolin is a political philosopher who coined the term Inverted Totalitarianism in 2003. He described what he saw as the emerging form of government in the United States. The United States is turning into a managed democracy, where the government wants to control life aspects. Every natural resource and human being is commodified and exploited by large corporations or Big Tech, to manipulate the citizens into surrendering their liberties and rights.

Rod Dreher's book called <u>Live Not by Lies</u> is an excellent book about the coming of Soft Totalitarianism. Dreher believes America is in a pre-totalitarian condition that is on the verge of becoming a full-blown form of Totalitarianism, which he calls Soft Totalitarianism. Dreher believes this new Totalitarianism will differ from the Hard Totalitarianism of Nazi Germany and the Soviet Union. These two regimes killed millions of people and put many people in concentration camps or gulags.

Soft Totalitarianism will be much gentler and more noninvasive. Soft Totalitarianism will arrive like a thief in the night—or what I call, Incognito Totalitarianism. One day, Americans will wake up and suddenly realize they have been captured and have lost all semblance of what America used to be—the land of the free. Compliance will not be by a government or dictator, but by a small group of elite people, large corporations, national news media, and through the power of visual social media and Big Tech. These people control and use the power of visual communication.

The new Totalitarianism is based on the ideology of classic liberalism, but with a new progressive radical creed known as *social justice*. Individual identity is replaced in favor of group identity based on gender, race, and sexuality diversity. You can choose to be any one of a thousand different sexes or genders, depending on how you feel that day. You will need to sign a diversity statement stating all these things, in order to work for any large corporation.

The wide extended use of flat screens over the last couple of decades is preparing America for this transition. The widespread loneliness and social atomization, decreasing religious status, loss of respect for institutions, willingness to believe the lies and propaganda, feelings over truth, desire for utopia, extreme liberal educators, and the willingness to transgress and destroy has been spread through the power of visual communication. In the past, intellectuals have been the revolutionaries. It is no different in America today, as college-educated elites are at the forefront of social justice and advocacy. Many of the people protesting are young women from wealthy and middle-class families. Social justice is replacing religion in the younger generations.

As discussed earlier, Digital Totalitarianism or Surveillance Capitalism is contributing to the process of change in America. People are willing to be followed and watched for convenience and entertainment. Americans are turning over their lives to Big Tech.

The new Totalitarianism, by whatever name you wish to apply—soft, digital, inverted, or incognito—is an extreme danger to the life lived in America. Totalitarianism seeks to reshape the character of individuals. The goal is to make everyone the same. Individualism needs to be replaced with groups. Eliminate institutions, tear down statues and history, eliminate standards and truth, and remove faith and religion. They hope that the last vestiges of family life and close friendships become distant, lost memories. The radical left controls education in the schools of our young people. Religion is being pushed away into a deep dark corner.

It is clear today that between socialism and communism, there is no difference. Both lead to a condition of affairs in which the State counts for everything and the individual for nothing. It is impossible to build up a healthy society based on class envy and class hatred. Without God and family as the primary focus of life, society and culture will disintegrate. No one is to be favored over anyone else in employment, housing, education, and welfare in the new State. Demand for free everything will eventually empty the public's purse. The cultural consequences will be dependency, crime, squalor, and hopelessness. The sad thing is—that through the power of visual communication, a significant number of Americans will welcome this change. America actually voted for this draconian way of life in the 2020 election, as the radical far left was supported by all institutions I have been discussing.

During the hearing for Judge Amy Coney Barrett for the 7th Circuit, Senator Dianne Feinstein accused her of being too Christian. Feinstein said, "Why is it that so many of us on this side have this very uncomfortable feeling that—you know, dogma and law are two different things. And I think whatever a religion is, it has its own dogma. The law is totally different. And I think in your case, Professor, when you read your speeches, the conclusion one draws is that the dogma lives loudly within you—and that is of concern when you come to big issues that large numbers of people have fought for years in this country."

All of the national news media organizations supported Feinstein's questioning of Barrett. The people on the left fear religion and the power that religion plays in the family and society.

Many people may not be concerned with this new thought process in America and believe that it is only the new fad of political correctness. A minority of people are trying to change over an indifferent and uninformed majority. Some of the majority laugh at the protesters and label them as *snowflakes*. Why are these people trying to change society? Who are the oppressors causing all the pain and injustice? They are the white, male, Anglo-Saxon, heterosexual, Christian, and white supremacists. If you are white and Christian, you are a white supremacist. According to these people, it does not matter whether you think you are or not—you are a white supremacist period. Oprah Winfrey, pro-athletes, and others who are multi-millionaires and billionaires are the oppressed.

Why is this happening now? Many times, for change to happen, a war, economic depression, a drought, or a pandemic (Covid-19) may be the catalyst for revolution. Totalitarianism appeals to fairness and a yearning for a utopian society, where everyone is taken care of and all are the same blissful selves. On the surface, it looks like peaceful and kind people caring for others, while it serendipitously supports rioting, burning down buildings, and looting businesses.

It is difficult for many people in America to see the breadth and depth of the secular world's relentless campaign to change the world. They are clever to smile and act like they care, while tearing down America's culture and religion. In Orwell's book, <u>Nineteen Eighty-Four</u>, he wrote:

> *He picked up the children's history book and looked at the portrait of Big Brother, which formed its frontispiece. The hypnotic eyes gazed into his own. It was as though some huge force was pressing down upon you—something that penetrated inside your skull, battering against your brain, frightening you out of your beliefs, persuading you, almost, to deny the evidence of your senses. In the end the Party would announce that two and two made five, and you would have to believe it. It was inevitable that they should make that claim sooner or later: the logic of their position demanded it. Not merely the validity of experience, but the very existence of external reality, was tacitly denied by their philosophy. The heresy of heresies was common sense. And what was terrifying was not that they would kill you for thinking otherwise, but that they might be right. For, after all, how do we know that two and*

two make four? The party told you to reject the evidence of your eyes and ears. It was their final, most essential command. Day and night the telescreens bruised your ears with statistics. Everything faded into mist. The past was erased, the erasure was forgotten, the lie became truth.

The new Totalitarian State aims to not only control everything you do, but also fill your mind with the beliefs, thoughts, and emotions of their choosing. The left will keep spuing their propaganda on everyone's flat screen, until they turn everyone to their side. Do not underestimate their resolve and the power of visual communication. They are slowly blinding you to true or ultimate reality!

Let us look into the future as to how America may look with all the flat screens and technology. You wake up in the morning to the alarm on your smartphone. Big Tech now knows when you set the alarm to go to bed, the time you woke up in the morning, and where you were sleeping. You shower and eat breakfast. Your smart refrigerator records what you are eating and makes a shopping list for you to use in the future. As you leave the house to go to work, the thermostat is set to the government set temperature when you are not home. The computer-driven car you lease drives you to work. The camera in the vehicle captures the title of the book you are reading on the way to work. The camera follows your facial reactions, while you are reading the book. The computer in your office monitors the work you do for the day. It tracks all the websites you visit, emails, tweets, and other posts. After work, you tell your car you would like to stop at a local watering hole on the way home. You have a glass of wine and pay for it with your smartphone. The phone logs your transaction and the name of the wine you drank. You arrive at home. The temperature is automatically set to the Government allowed temperature while you are home.

The refrigerator records what you have for dinner. You have had two cheeseburgers and a steak this week. You have gone over your allowed beef intake for the week. Beef is going to be removed from your grocery list this week. You know that the State is reducing the number of cattle in the United States, because they are expelling too much methane gas into the environment. Someone from Big Brother, or maybe, in this case, Big Sister, will be coming to your home to re-educate you on your diet allowances.

You turn on the TV. The camera in the TV watches and records your reactions to the programs and commercials you are watching. You must make sure you smile anytime Big Brother puts anything on the flat screen. You do not want to acquire any demerits for not supporting the hierarchy. You get ready for bed and set your alarm.

All your actions and responses to everything you observed during the day have been recorded and analyzed by artificial intelligence software. You will be exposed to the things Big Tech knows you will respond to the next day. If your attitudes and actions were not what was expected of you, you will need re-training from the people who take care of you. Big Brother wants you to live the life that they desire and believe is best for you. You have been programmed—and many people will be completely unaware of it.

Technology is not that far away from accomplishing that type of surveillance. What is Alexa recording in your home now? As we have known it, life in America will not survive the coming of a new totalitarian regime, unless the Church steps up to the plate and rescues the family. There needs to be a spiritual awakening or revival in America. Do not let the power of visual communication and the secular world change you, blind you, and cause you to drift away from your faith and your family.

> *Propaganda works best when those who are being manipulated are confident that they are acting on their own free will.*
>
> — Joseph Goebbels

Chapter 8

Training Your Vision and Perception

1 Corinthians 13:12 NLT

Now we see things imperfectly, like puzzling reflections in a mirror, but then we will see everything with perfect clarity.

Sight is what you see with your eyes,
Vision is what you see with your mind.

— Robert Kiyosaki

In Chapter 2, you learned about the miracle of vision and how unique, complex, and intricate the vision process is. This miracle allows us to marvel at the beautiful universe that God created. Your vision involves more than fifty percent of your brain function. It takes an enormous amount of processing by the brain, to create what you see and then judge what you see in milliseconds. Your brain performs one hundred trillion calculations per second. Yes, I said trillions of calculations per second through one hundred trillion connections in the brain.

The human eye can see eight million colors, though you would not know it by how men dress. Your eyes are seeing continually,

153

without you being conscious of it. You are only consciously aware of an exceedingly small portion of what your eyes observe. Many things pass through your vision that you are entirely unaware of seeing. Most of what your eyes are watching is subconscious. These subconscious images that your mind stores, do affect your paradigm over time. Because of the volume of information going into your mind, your paradigm and biases will slowly and automatically change over time. A significant emotional event can change your paradigm very quickly.

By the time you are six years of age, your vision has developed to its mature state. Up until recently, scientists believed that you could not improve your vision after the age of six. The brain has plasticity or the ability to learn new skills throughout your life. Recent advances in research and technology are available to enhance the quality of your vision, regardless of age. You can teach an old dog new tricks! You can learn to ride a bicycle at an older age, even if you have never ridden a bike before. It may take you longer than when you were younger, but your brain and body can be trained to ride a bicycle. The sharpness of your vision or acuity can be improved later in life by a small percentage. You can train your mind to see and perceive the world around you from an exciting and new perspective. There are different computer programs available to you, in addition to vision training that you can do on your own.

Vision and perception go hand in hand. Sight is measured by looking at specific sized letters at a determined distance. Perception is the ability to take what your eyes see, process the information, and actively make sense of the image received. Perceptional learning forms essential foundations of complex cognitive processes. Aside from the classic five senses, there are other types of perception. These are spatial perception, form perception, thermal perception, proprioception, and time perception, to name a few. Perception is an extremely complicated process. It is an active process of selection, organization, and interpretation. Examples of perceptional learning are what radiologists do in their residency to look at X-rays, MRIs, and CT scans. In ophthalmology, doctors are trained to recognize eye diseases by looking at a person's retina. I can see things in a retina that an untrained person could not see. A pathologist looks through a microscope and scans the slide for any abnormalities in the biopsy. A significant portion of the training doctors go through is related to perception.

Perceptual learning occurs continuously in everyday life. Experience shapes the way people see and gradually forms and modifies their paradigm. This learning leads to significant issues about sensory experiences ontology—the relationship between cognition and perception. The prevalent idiom that *practice makes perfect* captures the essence of the ability to reach impressive perceptual skills. The area of the brain, responsible for the particular function you are training, will increase in cortical volume. Expert musicians have larger auditory areas in their brains.

Why do people make mistakes in their perception? In most cases, it is not that they have diminished vision. Many people just go through life and do not pay much attention to the world around them. They are self-absorbed in their lives. Another reason (as I said earlier) is that the brain is processing trillions of sensory data information per second. You are only conscious of a small fraction of the sensory input. Many times, when your mind is not entirely focused on a situation, your brain fills in the gaps from your paradigm or previous experiences. Many times, your brain does not fill in the information with the correct data. Your perception is wrong, based on the information your paradigm sent to the visual processing center in your brain.

During an emotional event, your emotions can alter your perception remarkably. Your limbic nervous system overrides the decision-making portion of the brain. Your emotions allow your bias or paradigm to misinterpret the scene or event. Eyewitnesses to a crime are wrong many times. Unfortunately, many people have been imprisoned or executed, because the eye witness' paradigm caused them to see the crime incorrectly.

Most mistakes are human errors. Almost all plane crashes are pilot errors—and nearly all car crashes are human errors. Systemic biases or your paradigm make you prone to commit errors or mistakes. Your expectations shape the way you perceive the world. Your paradigm or biases are unconscious responses, in most cases. Everyone is biased—you just do not know it or refuse to accept it. You also tend to access a situation quickly. This rapid-fire analysis causes you to miss many details. You think that you have correctly evaluated the scene and have not missed anything. But many times, you have not observed things as they are. Quick first impressions can be very misleading. With the hectic life that is present today, everyone is prone to making more mistakes.

You see a fraction of what you think you see. You and I do a lot of skimming in our daily lives, because we are so busy and distracted. You see what you expect to see or your paradigm conditions you to see things as your experience dictates. You may become so set in your beliefs that you become blind to a new idea or a more straightforward solution. Typical perception by people is economical—you only notice a portion of what your eyes see, as your attention waxes and wanes throughout the day. Although everyone thinks they are paying attention and that they see correctly. When you think you are good at something and are in an automatic mode, you tend to lose focus. You are driving down the road and arrive at your destination, but you do not remember the details of driving there. This tendency for periods of inattention leads to more flawed perceptions and mistakes.

The Oakland Raiders Pro Football team has a reputation for being the dirtiest and most penalized professional football team. Is it really true or are there other factors in play? A research study was done where trained referees were shown a tape of an aggressively played staged football game. In one tape, the team wearing the white uniforms were the aggressive players. In the other video, the team wearing the black uniforms were the aggressive players. Half of the referees watched the tape with the white uniform players being aggressive—and the other half watched the aggressive black uniform team. The referees who watched the black uniform team rated the play as aggressive and deserving of penalties, more than the white-uniformed team. The color black modified the referee's opinion of the aggressive play in the game.

A review of the Oakland Raiders' penalties shows that they are significantly more penalized than the NFL team average. Did the Oakland Raiders, over the past many years, play more aggressively and receive more penalties? Did the color of their uniforms contribute to the number of penalties? Teams may wish not to have black-colored uniforms, as they are going to be penalized more often. The context in which you are viewing a scene, such as color, is crucial. It influences or changes your perception.

You can improve your vision and perception with training. RevitalVision is a perceptual learning program based on visual stimulation. The term *perceptual learning* describes a process, whereby practicing specific tasks leads to an improvement in visual performance. It has been shown that visual performance improves with repetitive practice on specific controlled visual tasks. The typical building block of the visual stimulus in the field of neuroscience is the Gabor Patch.

The Gabor Patch activates and matches the receptive areas in the brain's vision center. A Gabor Patch looks like a series of black and white bars. They can be oriented in a variety of ways. They can be easily discernable or challenging to see, small or large, central or peripheral, and rotating or stationary. The RevitalVision software program uses Gabor Patches to stimulate the vision centers in the brain. The program improves neuronal efficiency and improves contrast sensitivity in the visual cortex.

Contrast sensitivity is a more complex and refined determination of vision quality. Contrast testing involves looking at a slightly lighter color of grey symbols, with a somewhat different shade of a grey background. It takes a more refined level of vision than seeing black letters on a white background.

Another way to describe vision and perception is called *visual intelligence*. There are two excellent books about visual intelligence. Ann Marie Seward Barry wrote the book, <u>Visual Intelligence,</u> with the subtitle, <u>Perception, Image, and Manipulation in Visual Communication</u>. A second book, <u>Visual Intelligence,</u> with the subtitle <u>Sharpen Your Perception, Change Your Life</u>, is written by Amy E. Herman.

Dictionary.com defines intelligence as *the capacity for learning, reasoning, understanding, and similar forms of mental activity, aptitude in grasping truths, facts, and meanings.* Visual intelligence refers to a person's ability to perceive, analyze, and understand visual information in the world around them. Other terms are discernment, savvy, skill, knowledge, comprehension, and cleverness.

People tend to live their daily lives and do not pay too much attention to what they look at on a given day. They superficially accept what they see. As you learned previously, this can be extremely dangerous. Nearly all the things you are observing on flat screens are manipulated for ulterior motives. Flat screens dominate everyone's lives. Braden and Hortin suggest that visual literacy is the ability to understand and to use images. Visual literacy includes the ability to think, learn, and express oneself in terms of images. Two essential skills are needed—awareness of the logic, emotion, and attitudes suggested in the visual message and the ability to produce meaningful images for communication with others. What is needed is recognizing attitudes, beliefs, and true meanings embedded within and between images on flat screens or visual intelligence.

Visual intelligence means observing differently, seeing what is behind the images, looking more abstractly, and looking into the images' reasons. Visual intelligence is a system of looking at the world around us with a critical analyzing awareness that can be trained and developed to lead you towards perfect perception. With the world dominated by images on flat screens, everyone must improve their visual intelligence or the ability to examine, understand, and perceive the meaning of the propaganda behind the images.

The eye is an incredible organ that provides you with the ability to see this world that God has made. When you look at a flat screen, you may only perceive or understand sixty or seventy percent of what you are watching. Many things may affect your perception. Your emotional state, mindset, prior experience, current alertness, and paradigm will determine your reality of what you are viewing.

Superficially, you assume that what you are watching is honest and true. You trust that your senses have interpreted the images correctly. If what you are watching triggers an emotional response in your amygdala, your frontal lobe's cognitive process is attenuated. Visual intelligence and perfect perception depend on the areas of your brain functioning correctly. The brain tends to initially accept your first impression of what you are viewing as true and real.

You may feel that your mind is in control, making judicious and rational decisions in a relatively unbiased manner, but the opposite may be true. You may cruise along without any critical examination of reality and can be continually fooled. Numerous studies show that you do not see what is there, but you are preconditioned to see what you want to see and expect to see. That is why editing is so difficult, because you will read what a sentence is meant to say, even if there is a word or two missing. So, if you find an error, please be kind. I paid for an editor to find my mistakes, but editing is challenging.

The images you are observing are manipulated continuously to influence you. Techniques such as lighting, shadow, and color are incorporated into the images in a specific manner. The first time I shot a TV commercial, the expert marketing person I hired took three hours just to set up the lighting, shadows, and color for the thirty-second shot. I was amazed at the time and detail involved in producing such a short segment.

False and misleading images are why everyone must develop their visual intelligence. Visual intelligence gives you a more precise and more in-depth understanding of whether you can trust your perception and an appreciation of how flat screens attempt to alter your beliefs and values. Chaos theorist, Roger vonOech, believes that everyone has a *right answer mentality* deeply ingrained. It causes you to accept the first opinion that fits and stops you from looking for the optimum answer.

An image reaches the amygdala (your center for emotions) before you have time to determine the image's nature cognitively. This pathway is related to the flight or fight response. If something is dangerous, you want to react to that danger immediately.

Humans tend to think in images or visual thinking. When you try to solve a problem, you visually think about how to solve the problem. You only write the answer after you have visualized how to remedy the situation. Inventors think visually to develop their inventions. Visual communication is compelling. It connects to the way you think. Understanding the power of visualization was made popular with the publication of The Power of Positive Thinking by Norman Vincent Peale. He proposed using visualization to create a positive image of achievement. All professional golfers use visualization to hit a golf shot. The ability to visualize a golf shot improves the likelihood of hitting a great shot.

Manipulating images is designed to alter your perception of the image or video. Research has shown four main zones of comfort in the relationship to your environment—intimate distance, personal distance, social distance, and public distance. An intimate distance is from contact to eighteen inches. You are close enough to see physically expressed emotion, but you are so close that you cannot see clearly, nor see the rest of the person's body and how the rest of their body reacts.

Personal distance is from eighteen inches to four feet. This distance allows for personal contact, but you can read expressions clearly and see body movements. Trust is a major factor at this distance, because of the inability to react quickly to someone's actions. Social distance is from four feet to twelve feet. This distance does not allow for touch and marks a limit of domination. Public distance is from twelve feet and beyond. It is characterized by non-involvement. At this distance, you can easily detect and respond to other people's movements. When a zone is inappropriately violated, you feel uneasy, anxious, and possibly threatened. Proxemics can be used in images to alter your opinion of someone or an event.

Another method of manipulating perception is through the use of color. Color can cause an emotional response and an association from past experiences. Yellow corresponds to earth, green to the sea, blue to the sky, and red to fire are general associations. Colors are thought to have an associated temperature. Red, orange, and yellow are warm colors. Blue, green, and violet are cool colors. You will generally feel warmer in a room painted red. Color can also portray a sense of softness and smoothness, such as pink looks soft. Colors add dimension to an image, as well.

The color yellow is associated with the debasement of gold and portrays jealousy and disloyalty. A painting by Van Dyck shows Judas wearing a yellow cloak. Nazi Germany had the Jewish people wear yellow Stars of David on their clothes. The color blue has a calming effect and is used in rooms where a calm atmosphere is wanted. Orange light has been shown to reduce muscle tone. Red is the color for action. You see many male politicians wearing a red tie to stimulate you for action, such as voting for them.

The use of lighting changes perception, such as bringing out shadows. Lighting from above can portray goodness and a halo effect. Camera angles play a significant role in manipulating opinions. A camera at eye level is natural and depicts equality or neutrality. If the camera angle is below eye level, you are looking up at the image or person. This camera angle gives you the sensation of importance—or you look up to the person. Increasing the severity of the angle can increase the perception of increased power and authority. Just the opposite is also true. If the camera angle is above the image, you are looking down on an image or person, and they seem inferior or less worthy. As the angle increases, you may sense terror or a menacing feeling. Camera angles manipulate your perception of the images you are viewing.

As discussed with proxemics, distance added to these other features compounds the effect. When the camera comes in for a closeup, the person becomes more interesting and relevant. The facial features portrays emotions, inner thoughts, and a sense of personal connection to the person. If the distance is extremely close, it can have the opposite effect, resulting in invading your personal space and intimidating. Closely related to distance is the size of an image. Larger images denote importance and authority.

Nearly every image, movie, or video has been manipulated, for a purpose that may not be easily seen or understood. You are now aware of many psychological factors that modify your perception of things you see—such as color, lighting, distance, size, and texture. These techniques are framed and portrayed in a specific context, chosen to modify your beliefs and thoughts. No flat-screen image occurs without manipulation through planning, editing, and framing.

The most obvious form of manipulation is content, which is edited to meet their objectives. Every word is dissected, discussed, and analyzed for effect before it is heard or shown. With new technology, images that you are watching live can be manipulated in real time. It is difficult to know to what extent transmissions are trustworthy and reliable. It is not whether images on flat screens are manipulated, but whether you can see through their propaganda.

Think about the images or videos you have seen on TV of President Obama and President Trump. Do you remember ever seeing a photo of President Obama where he was not smiling? The images are framed perfectly with the proper lighting, size, angle, and distance. How about images of President Trump? Were the images framed, sized, and angled to promote him, and was he always smiling? Seldom did the news outlets ever present a nice picture of President Trump. Maybe they even made the images with extra orange color to make him look like the umpa lumpas. All flat screen images are presented in a manner to influence your perception.

Advertising is the art of arresting the intelligence long enough to get money out of it.

— Stephen Leacock

Now that you have an idea about some of the vast number of ways images on flat screens can alter your thoughts, beliefs, culture, and faith in Jesus Christ, you can train and develop a clearer vision and better perception. I think Sherlock Holmes is a great place to start. You should consider reading some of the Sherlock Holmes books to get the gist of how his mind worked.

You see, but do not observe

The world is full of obvious things which nobody by any chance observes. It has long been an axiom of mine that the little things are infinitely the most important.

— Sherlock Holmes

Sherlock Holmes is famous for his reasoning capabilities and investigative techniques. He was extremely skilled in the analysis of trace evidence. Many times, Holmes used a magnifying glass at the scene to examine the evidence. He employed deductive reasoning as a method for observing details. His guiding principle was The Sign of Four, which says, *When you have eliminated the impossible, whatever remains, however improbable, must be the truth.* So, put on your Sherlock Holmes hat and let us see what we can find.

I have a friend who is in the FBI. I discussed my thoughts about perception with him, and he told me a story about his FBI training. The FBI does an extensive amount of observational skill training. He was in class with other trainees. Suddenly, a person opened the door and fired a gun into the classroom. (The person had fired a gun with blanks.) Immediately, the teacher told everyone to settle down, as this was part of their training. Then they were told that it was a test. They were to write down everything they could remember about the incident, down to the tiniest detail.

The tendency is for the human mind to skim over things in life. As I said previously, the mind is being bombarded every day with information. The mind is also occupied with images on flat screens for a significant amount of time each day. Disciplining your mind to observe details will lead you to better vision, observation, and true reality.

The famous disease pioneer, Louis Pasteur, stated, "Chance only favors the prepared mind." The neuroscientist, Wilfred Trotter, said, "Knowledge comes from noticing resemblances and recurrences in the events that happen around us." W.I.B. Beveridge published the book The Art of Scientific Investigation. He said that the art of observation is not passively watching, but is an active process. One cannot observe everything closely. Therefore one must discriminate and try to select the significant. Training in observation follows the same principles as training in any activity. At first, one must do things consciously and laboriously—then a habit is established.

French physiologist, Claude Bernard, stated there are two types of observation—(a) spontaneous or passive observations, which are unexpected, and (b) induced or active observations, which are deliberately sought. Effective spontaneous observation involves first noticing some object or event. The thing noticed will only become significant, if the observer's mind either consciously or unconsciously relates it to some relevant knowledge or past experience—or if in pondering on it, he arrives at some hypothesis. What is more important and more difficult, is observing resemblances or correlations between things that appear entirely unrelated on the surface.

Radiologists, dermatologists, pathologists, and ophthalmologists depend on their observational skills to make a diagnosis. It takes years of training to determine if there is a subtle disease present. Still, as humans, we all make mistakes. The Harvard Medical School did a study with radiologists to evaluate their observation skills. The researchers placed an image of a two-inch gorilla on the side of a chest X-ray. They then asked the radiologist to examine the

X-Ray for cancerous nodules. Eighty-three percent of radiologists missed the gorilla shaking its fist at them on the X-Ray. They were examining the X-Ray for cancer lesions and therefore were prone to missing the gorilla. The gorilla did not have the structural characteristics of a cancer lesion, so it was ignored. When you are concentrating diligently on a specific thing, you can miss other obvious things.

I give talks about paradigms related to the first book I published called Believing is Seeing—the subtitle is Focus Through a God Centered Paradigm. I gave a talk at a church breakfast with over one hundred men in attendance about how perception and paradigms work. I showed a PowerPoint with ten playing cards. Four of the cards were the wrong color, such as a red five of clubs and a black ten of hearts. The cards were shown in about one second intervals. I asked them how many cards they saw by raising their hands as I called out different numbers of cards. A couple of men raised their hands at four cards, with the vast majority claiming they saw six or seven cards. No one saw all ten cards. The reason is that the brain did not count the wrong colored cards, because there is no such thing as a red five of clubs!

I knew many of the men in attendance. I gave them a hard time about not counting a few cards. I was setting them up for the video I was going to show them next. I told them that I would show them a short video and admonished them to do a better job counting. They were going to see a video of three girls in black shirts, passing a basketball to each other as they walked around on a stage. There would be three girls in white shirts doing the same thing. They were to count how many times the girls in the white shirts passed the ball to each other. The girls could also fake a pass or bounce a pass.

The girls crisscrossed back and forth for about thirty seconds. At that time, one of the girls in a black shirt near the screen's edge left the stage. As she left the scene, a person in a gorilla suit entered the scene. The gorilla walked to the center of the stage and beat its chest. Afterward, all the girls and the gorilla left the stage. I asked the men how many times did the girls in the white shirts passed the ball? They proudly and quickly told me sixteen times. I said, "OK, you got that right, but how many of you saw the gorilla?" They were shocked and thought there was no way there was a gorilla in the video. I replayed the video again, and they all saw the gorilla! They accused me of playing a different video. Only ten men out of more than one hundred men saw the gorilla!

In most cases, about fifty percent of people see the gorilla. I increased the effect by using the cards first and suggesting they watch the girls in the white shirts closely. You can influence someone to see what you want them to see.

There was a famous experiment where a person asked another person on the street for directions. While giving the directions, two men carrying a large sign or poster walked between them. Another person was behind the sign. As they passed in front of the person giving the instructions, the person behind the sign replaced the person receiving the directions. After the sign passed, less than fifty percent of the people giving the instructions, noticed a different person in front of them.

As you have already read, if you repeat propaganda lies enough times, it will become the truth. The paradigm present at the time of seeing an image or event, will cause you to see what your paradigm says you are to see, even in the presence of a different fact or truth. Training your vision and perception will help you develop a different paradigm. It will be more open and have the ability to see more clearly.

Think about what things are influencing your life or have influenced your life that compose your paradigm. The most important factor is your faith or lack of faith in Jesus Christ. That alone will be the most significant factor in your paradigm. Other factors include family, education, where you grew up, friends, job or profession, dreams, hopes, desires, wealth or money, morals, ethics, media sources, health, age, government, and politics.

People will always see the same image or event differently, because everyone's paradigm is unique to them. What you observe in life is unique to you. Every event, image, and incident in your life, consciously and subconsciously contributes to and alters your paradigm. That is why you must be careful about the things you expose yourself to—what you see, what you study, your friends, or situations in your environment.

Amy E. Herman is an attorney and art historian. She uses art to train people to improve their perception. She teaches people at the FBI, the Department of Defense, medical students, Fortune 500 companies, and many others. Just like the Highlights Magazine picture, you can train your vision with art, computer programs, and other techniques. Training your vision by critically observing art can help you pay attention to details. The Journal of the American Medical Association published a study that showed studying art improved diagnostic and observational skills. You need to be Sherlock Holmes, while observing a piece of art. This training of your mind will become more automatic with repetition.

Herman recommends this exercise—look at a painting with many details for one minute. Just like the FBI trainees, write down every small detail you can remember. Look at the object and see how you did. The next time look at an image for three minutes, do the same thing. Compare your results. Do this exercise on a routine basis and you will notice an improvement in your observation skills. The more you train yourself to continually observe the environment around you, the process of critical observation will become routine.

You need to think about these five Ws when evaluating something. They are the basics of observation and perception—who, what, where, when, and why. Other considerations about what you see or watch on a flat screen are: Is there an underlying agenda? Does the source have a reliable reputation for truthfulness and honesty? Is the presentation truthful? Can you find other reliable information to back it up? Be careful about first impressions. Do the facts match past expectations?

If you observe a piece of art (or anything in life), you need to be very descriptive and detailed oriented. Do not say something is large, but measure it if possible or give a scale for comparison. Do not assume anything when critically examining something. Expect the unexpected and look for any pattern that seems out of order. Be willing to look from different perspectives. Is there anything out of place or missing? The absence of something might be critical, as well. A significant negative can be vital in making the correct medical diagnosis. We all have unconscious biases—and you need to be careful about letting those affect how you observe things. You need to recognize any unconscious biases you may have, so you can keep those out of your perceptions.

When you evaluate a piece of art, it is essential to follow a logical observation method. It is good to start by observing the image or piece of art in its entirety, to get a general idea about what you are examining. Then divide the image into sections or quadrants, depending on how much detail is in the image. By focusing on a small area, you can discover intricate details.

When I was taking flying lessons, my instructor told me to watch the horizon for any other planes, by looking at one clock hour at a time. You make sure there is no plane in that clock hour and go to the next clock hour. Scanning back and forth is not the best way to spot a tiny object on the horizon. Focus on one clock hour at a time and then go to the next clock hour until you have covered the horizon. Then start over.

Practice your observation skills on this famous piece of art. First, write down your observations and let us see how you did. Maybe you can add to the description of the things I have described in this famous painting.

Arrangement in Grey and Black No 1
Whistler's Mother
James McNeill Whistler (1871)

What do you think about this famous painting? There is a compelling stillness to it. It has a minimalist portrayal and geometric austerity. She is rigid and erect, wearing long black clothes that you might wear at a funeral. Her appearance is icy and is accentuated by the black and grey colors. She and the dark-colored chair are facing to the left and away from the artist. She is wearing a white lace cap or bonnet that drapes past her shoulders that could be tied. This type of head covering would be common in the era of the late 1800s. Her dress sleeves have lace cuffs. Her hands are folded in her lap, clutching a white handkerchief. There is a rectangular painting on the wall with a scene of buildings behind a field. At the right top corner is the black edge of, what appears to be, a picture frame. Her head is not quite an equal distance between the frames. Her head is slightly titled down. She appears to be gazing slightly upward, staring at something somewhat higher than her eye level.

On the left side of the painting is a black, vertically hanging drapery. There is a white, intricate, subtle pattern in the drapery. The back wall has a matte grey appearance with a large dark baseboard. The wood flooring is running vertically in the painting. Her feet are sitting on a footrest. Her shoes would be considered basic or plain and do not match the status of the rest of her attire. Are there any other observations you would make about this famous painting?

Let us do some further vision training, by finding animals in a couple of pictures. Many animals rely on camouflage to hide from predators. Some predators depend on camouflage to get close to their prey.

There is a wolf in two of the pictures and an antelope in the other picture.

What other things can you train yourself to observe in this world? You can learn to read other people. There are two excellent books about body language. <u>What Everybody Is Saying</u> by FBI agent Joe Navarro and <u>You Say More Than You Think</u> by Janine Driver are excellent books, if you are interested in learning to read body language? I will go over some of the basics to get you started.

When you finally pull away from your flat screen, you will be interacting with people from all kinds of cultures and beliefs. You do not always understand what they are thinking or are planning to do. Suppose you do not have well-developed observation skills. In that case, you may fail at a job interview, lose a competitive sports game, fail in personal relationships, or many other vital things in life. If you develop your observation skills, you can have the upper hand. You can be one step ahead of everyone around you. Successful people have great observation ability. They can read a situation and react in a way that makes them successful.

Body language is learning to observe facial expressions, physical movements, posture, gestures, body distance or proxemics, touching, clothing, and body appearance. Body language is nonverbal communication. Nonverbal communication refers to facial expressions, tone of voice, gestures, eye contact or lack of eye contact, body language, posture, touching, and body adornment, such as jewelry, clothes, hairstyle, tattoos, etc.

UCLA Professor Albert Mehrabian and Susan R. Ferris published a study in the Journal of Consulting Psychology about nonverbal communication. They found that a message's meaning is 7% verbal, 38%, and 55% visual. The conclusion was that 93% of communication is nonverbal in nature.

Becoming proficient in reading body language is not about some abstract or neat topic. It is about how you are going to live and experience life. It will determine how successful you are in life. Developing the skill to read people requires constant training and a commitment to understanding people more thoroughly. It is beneficial with your friends, acquaintances, family, and especially your significant other.

The first rule in observing people is determining someone's baseline behavior and looking for changes in their normal behavior. All body language responses do not mean the same in everyone. There are basics, but you are looking for deviations from normal behavior. Paul Ekman wrote about seven similar universal facial emotions expressed by people: surprise, contempt, anger, disgust, fear, sadness, and happiness.

You need to study a person's normal body language signals, before evaluating any changes in their behavior. You should make a concerted effort to advance your observational skills. As I have said before, you need to put on your Sherlock Holmes' hat. Train yourself to distinguish between authentic and misleading signals. Different experts follow different techniques of observation. Some experts scan from the face down to the feet—others scan from the feet to the face. You choose what works best for you.

Paul Ekman estimated that there are ten thousand different facial expressions from the 42 muscles in the face. The face can be very revealing about a person's true sentiment. You are trained as a child to always smile when greeting someone, not make faces. Like my German grandmother told me, never ever let anyone know how you feel. It was great for playing sports. When I was young, as I was cool as a cucumber, no matter the situation during a sporting event. People look to the face to determine the feelings of another person. Many people will make sure they do not show any emotion on their faces.

Pacifying behaviors are excellent indicators of uncomfortableness. The first pacifying behavior you adopt as a baby is sucking your thumb. As you age, you develop more subtle ways of pacifying yourself. These displays are using your hands to soothe your stress. You stroke your neck, play with your hair, rub your forehead, or (in the case of President Bill Clinton during his deposition) you touch your nose. You physically use your hand to touch different parts of your body to pacify yourself, because you are uncomfortable.

People do not realize it, but your feet can reveal a lot about your feelings. If you walk up to someone or a group of people and they do not turn even slightly toward you, they do not want to talk with you. Another fundamental clue is where their belly button is pointed? If it is not turned toward you, they are not interested. Wherever your belly button goes, that is where your attention is projected. When playing defense in basketball, I always watch the opponent's belly button. They can do head fakes, shoulder fakes, and foot fakes, but they will only go wherever their belly button is going.

Feet and legs are a good indicator of a person's emotional state. Is the person shaking their leg when they are crossed? Do they have happy feet, which shows they are uneasy? When they cross their leg, did they cross the leg away from you or towards you? The way a person leans their torso or body reveals their feelings. You lean away from people that make you uncomfortable and lean toward someone you like.

The position of your arms can indicate your sentiment, such as crossed arms blocking your body. When you are upset or uncomfortable, you withdraw your arms. The spreading of your arms denotes a feeling of confidence. The power of a handshake can be revealing. One of the strongest hand gestures is the steepling of the hands, fingertip to fingertip. Steeples of different types signal confidence and authority. When placing your hands in something, such as a pocket, thumbs indicate confidence or uneasiness. Visible thumbs mean confidence; hidden thumbs reveal uneasiness or lack of confidence.

The arms, hands, legs, and feet provide reliable signals of a person's feelings or intentions. Facial features, though, can be deceiving at times. These are a few of the things to look for when interacting with people and determining their state of mind. If I have piqued your interest, reading the two recommended books on body language will increase your knowledge.

Training your vision and perception can be fun and enjoyable. If my wife and I sit waiting somewhere, such as an airport, we have fun trying to make up a story about another couple in the waiting area. We will never know who is correct, but it sharpens your observation skills as you pick out any tiny details of their actions and appearance.

If your biases or paradigm are clouding your vision or blinding you to reality, how do you get around it? First, you must have a desire to improve your vision and perception. With your newly acquired skills, you can become Sherlock Holmes and observe all the tiny details. Companies that specialize in paradigm training, begin by showing you how significantly your paradigm alters your perception. Once you understand the power of paradigms, you can learn to change your paradigm.

For a particular belief, solving a problem, forming or changing a company's mission plan, or developing a God-centered paradigm, you need to start with a zero paradigm. You need to get rid of all your previous knowledge or biases about a subject. Start with a clean slate. As it states in the Bible, you become a new creature or person when you become a Christian.

After you are a Christian, you are a new creature or person. Start with a zero paradigm, think about what you believe. The Bible states the characteristics of an ideal Christian life. You would want to incorporate the fruit of the Holy Spirit found in Galatians 5—love, joy, peace, patience, kindness, goodness, faithfulness, gentleness, and self-control—into your God-centered paradigm.

What other ideas or characteristics would be beneficial for living a Christian life? After you have listed all the new attributes and characteristics, prioritize them in order of significance. Start working on the characteristics at the top of your list. Develop these new thoughts or beliefs. Make a plan to complete the list. Being open to new information and strategies is vital to changing your paradigm and perception.

As a Christian, use your new skills from your vision training and perception. Remove the fog or veil that the secular world uses

to blind you. The eye receives the image, but your mind decides
what you are going to see or perceive.

The blind are never unperceptive,
but the unperceptive are always blind.

— Randi G. Fine

The only thing worse than being blind
is having sight but no vision.

— Helen Keller

Chapter 9
Ultimate Reality

Either you deal with what is the reality or you can be sure that the reality is going to deal with you.

— Alex Haley

It's funny how humans can wrap their mind around things and fit them into their version of reality.

— Rick Riordan

For the past 2,500 years, famous philosophers have written and debated the various aspects of truth and reality. Aristotle, Plato, Socrates, Cicero, Hume, Kant, Descartes, Kuhn, and many others have proposed their beliefs about the origin, meaning, reality, and destiny of humankind. Many have tried to use science, logic, and their own opinions. While they did explain some things well, the final decrees of many of them led to paradoxes and confusion.

When the mind's eye rests on objects illuminated by truth and reality, it understands and comprehends them and functions intelligently, but when it turns to the twilight world of change and decay, it can only form opinions, its vision is confused and its beliefs shifting, and it seems to lack intelligence.

— Plato

What is reality? According to The Free Dictionary, reality is—

- *The quality or state of being actual or true*

- *One, such as a person, an entity, or an event that is actual*

- *The totality of all things possessing actuality, existence, or essence*

- *That which exists objectively and in fact*

- *Reality is the state of the world as it really is rather than as you might want it to be*

Reality is the total aggregate of all that exists or is real objectively, in contrast to imaginary things. It is the reality of all things known and unknown. Ontological questions involve various philosophical disciplines, such as science, religion, mathematics, and philosophical logic. There are two fundamental realities—objective physical objects (Physicalism) and realities not composed of actual objects, but formed by the conscience (Idealism). An objective reality denotes that something materially exists independent of the mind. Subjective reality means that perceiving reality is developed in your mind and not on physical objects.

From the beginning of humankind, with the first flickers of self-awareness and consciousness, we have searched and contemplated our origin, the meaning of life, destiny, and reality. What is the nature of our universe? What is our place in the universe? Why are we here? What is the reality of our existence? Just as everyone has their own opinion, there are numerous theories, ideas, and philosophies about these questions. Most philosophers and scientists writing about reality fail to begin at the source of creation and reality—God. Science cannot and probably will never prove or reject the origin of creation and the basis for true or ultimate reality.

The universe did not randomly appear from nothing into a vast, complex, and intricately connected creation. There is no evidence that the universe started to be created, but failed several million or trillion times until the universe miraculously popped up correctly. There are no remnants of past attempts for creation that failed.

Psalm 33:6 NLV

The heavens were made by the word of the Lord.
All the stars were made by the breath of his mouth.

The omnipotent and all-powerful God just breathed into existence the universe. God is a star breather and galaxy former. The explosive force of the big bang and the gravity to match that force had to be 1 part in 10 to the 60th—or the universe would not exist. That is a lot of zeros. God had to be freakishly precise in His creation and design. He breathed out the largest star that is 1,500 times the size of our Sun. The size of Earth's orbit around our Sun is extremely small compared to the size of this single star. It is gigantic and 40,000 degrees hot. Compare this massive star to the smallest things in the universe that we know about. They are called *quarks* and *leptons* and are 43 million times smaller than a grain of sand.

Based on the miracle of vision alone covered in Chapter Two, the eye could have never formed by random development and evolution. Evolution has been proven wrong by many scientists, but you do not hear very much about it. The secular world wants to hold on to Darwin's Theory of Evolution and still teach it in our schools. Whenever a mutation occurs, the mutated process in an organism is diminished nearly 100% of the time, not improved. You cannot mutate your way up the evolutionary ladder. To perceive what reality is all about, you need to start from the beginning. You have no excuse not to recognize the origin of the universe. You can begin your search for reality through your mind and senses.

Romans 1:20 NLT

For ever since the world was created, people have seen the earth and sky. Through everything God made, they can clearly see his invisible qualities – his eternal power and divine nature. So they have no excuse for not knowing God.

I think that true reality should be called ultimate reality. Ultimate reality takes reality to a new level. Ultimate reality transcends the non-physical and the physical dimensions of the universe. Ultimate reality is the most all-inclusive reality, the most authentic reality, and is the origin of all things in this world or simply stated—Ultimate Reality is God. Since we are made in His image, you and I are His most important creation. Unlike God, you have a body or vessel that your soul and spirit live in, until you are raised to heaven. You and I also have other characteristics that God gave us. You have a rational thinking mind. You can plan, solve complex problems, and have a conscious knowing right from wrong.

The very nature of God's creation discloses His presence. Only a divine, all-powerful, and omnipotent God could create the universe. It is so richly diverse and yet so intimately and intricately interconnected at the same time.

Science without religion is dangerous, because it necessarily entails a mechanization of humanity and

consequent loss of individual autonomy and spirituality.
On the other hand, religion without science is powerless,
because it lacks an effective means through which to
actualize the ultimate reality. Science and religion must
work together harmoniously.

— Masao Abe

When scientists and the secular world profess their beliefs about reality, a scientific worldview serves as a disintegrating force in culture and society. Science brought disintegration to the world. The technical revolution brought dehumanization to the world. Humankind experiences life as fragmented and unbalanced. Flat screens have isolated people from other people. Religion has been separated from the rest of life that people live today. Unwarranted belief in science and technology has eliminated the Christian worldview from society and culture. The secular world is systematically making the Christian worldview irrelevant to living life. The Christian worldview may be alright in your private life (though that is in jeopardy as well), but is no longer accepted in the workplace, school, politics, or any activity outside of the front door of your home.

Many worldviews have developed over the centuries. A worldview is a belief or perspective of the reality of the world where you and I live. It is a comprehensive system of beliefs or opinions about the world, life, and the thoughts held inside your mind or paradigm. Everyone has a worldview. Your perception of reality is how you make sense of the world. Your worldview is the outward representation of your inward paradigm. A worldview is like a pair of eyeglasses that you use to see and understand the world clearly. If the eye doctor gives you the right prescription, you will see clearly. If the doctor gives you the wrong prescription, your vision will be blurred. Your perception of the ultimate reality in the world depends on you having the correct worldview or paradigm. Many people are blind to the presence of ultimate reality, but have excellent vision.

Arthur Holmes, the author of the book Contour of a World View, states that a world view should pass specific tests. First, it should be rational. It should not ask you to believe in contradictory things. Second, it should be supported by evidence. It should be consistent with what you observe. Third, it should give a satisfying comprehensive explanation of reality. It should be able to explain why things are the way they are. Fourth, it should provide a satisfactory basis for living. It should not leave you feeling compelled to borrow elements of another worldview to live in this world.

There are common components that should compose a worldview. First, something exists. The universe is objective and rational. It is predictable. Second, all people should have knowledge of absolutes. Many people deny that there are any absolutes, but to deny it is to assert it. Everyone seeks an infinite reference point. For ultimate reality, it is God. Third, two contradictory statements cannot both be right. This is a primary law of logic. Today, people that say someone is wrong are labeled intolerant, bigoted, or narrow-minded. Fourth, all people exercise faith. You presuppose certain things to be true without absolute proof. These are inferences or assumptions upon which you base your belief.

Philosophy deals with different aspects of reality—the nature of reality itself and the relationship between the mind and reality. Ontology is the study of being, existence, and reality and how they are interrelated. Epistemology is the philosophy of knowledge—whether it is possible to know what kind of knowledge is present and how you gain that knowledge. Metaphysics is a branch of philosophy dealing with abstract concepts of being, knowing, time, space, substance, identity, and cause. Philosophers, scientists, theorists, and many others have attempted their hand at reality and have formed various worldviews. The most prominent worldviews are Theism, Deism, Naturalism, Nihilism, Existentialism, Postmodernism, and Pantheism. Christian Theism, New Age Pantheism, and Naturalism are the most prominent worldviews in America today.

Theism believes in an infinite God Who created the universe from nothing. The three primary theistic religions in the world today are Christianity, Islam, and Judaism. Christian theism believes humankind is the unique creation of God. You are made in His image, truth is through divine revelation, and your moral values are an expression of an absolute moral being. The God of creation is a personal God—and only through faith in Jesus Christ is eternal life possible. Christian Theism was the dominant worldview in America until the last two generations.

Deism was a prominent worldview in the 18th Century. The Deist believes that God is the world's creator, but God has abandoned His creation to let it progress independently.

Naturalism and other similar worldviews, such as Materialism, Secular Humanism, and Postmodernism, are becoming dominant worldviews in America today. They believe that the objective material world is all that exists. There is no soul or spirit—and God is irrelevant. Everything can be explained by natural law. Progress and evolutionary change are inevitable. Education is the guide to life and science is the ultimate source of knowledge and morals. Truth is observed from the five senses. Morality is a matter of personal preference. Man is autonomous and self-centered.

Postmodernism is beginning to take the place of naturalism in the last two generations. Postmodernism believes that absolute truth does not exist—and your beliefs trump facts or the truth. This worldview is rampant on college campuses today. The United States Constitution is irrelevant and is not needed today.

Nihilism sees no value in reality. There is no such thing as knowledge, existence, or the meaning of life. Human values are baseless and life is meaningless.

New Age Pantheism or New Age Consciousness has become prominent over the last two generations, as well. Pantheism has been present in Eastern Cultures for centuries. It is in the previous half-century that it became popular in America. Pantheism believes that God is in everything, or everything is a part of God. Humankind is the ultimate reality and is spiritual and eternal. There are no distinctions between humans, animals, or the rest of creation. All is one or connected—and all is god. Therefore, all of us are gods. You are a part of reality. You can change your consciousness by discovering your divinity. Reaching the final level of godliness may take an infinite number of birth cycles, deaths, and rebirths. There is no absolute truth, as two conflicting views can both be true.

Many people living in this New Age worldview feel that perception of reality is what your mind says you see at a specific moment. Your perception is your reality. This idealist reality is a common colloquial usage—that reality is developed from perceptions, feelings, beliefs, and attitudes forming your reality.

There is no reality beyond your perceptions and beliefs that you have about reality. Statements like—Perception is reality. My reality is not your reality. Life is how you see reality.—are believed by many people. Unfortunately, this is very superficial and can be deleterious to the person holding this understanding of reality. A famous neuroscientist, Oliver Sacks, stated that everything you experience is only a version of reality—a regulated, reliable hallucination you are accustomed to believing. According to Sacks, reality is only happening in your mind. What you are perceiving is only a representation of the real world.

Many educated people believe it is that simple. The only problem is that your perception may be completely wrong. You might say that it is OK, since it is my perception and my life. Let's say you are visiting Yellowstone National Park. You stop your car to look at the beautiful scenery. As you get out of the car, you see a furry animal running toward you. You think that it is a cute puppy dog. Instead, it is an angry grizzly bear running toward you. I think you would want to know the difference. This story may sound a little outrageous. How can I see a grizzly bear and you see a puppy dog? Unfortunately, many people with non-Christian worldviews see things in life that are just as absurdly incorrect. A diminished level of vision, perception, and reality has caused many problems for people throughout humankind's history. They are blinded to the presence of ultimate reality.

> *Since we cannot change reality,*
> *let us change the eyes which see reality.*
>
> — Nikos Kazantzakis

The phrase *perception is reality* is attributed to political strategist Lee Atwater. You may remember him as the political advisor to President George H.W. Bush in the late 1980s. He used this idea when talking about the importance of public relations in campaigns. Just like Hitler and Stalin, you can control the narrative, if you can control people's perceptions.

Perceiving reality has to do with your paradigm and perception, which can lead to a false reality. In sports, a referee makes a call. The team's fans who feel they got an incorrect call are absolutely sure they were robbed of a championship—only to have instant replay verify they were wrong. Misperceptions happen continually all day long.

2 Corinthians 4:3-4 NIV

And even if our gospel is veiled, it is veiled to those who are perishing. The god of this age has blinded the minds of unbelievers, so that they cannot see the light of the gospel that displays the glory of Christ, who is the image of God.

Can science get us closer to ultimate reality? Quantum mechanics is a branch of physics dealing with the very small. In classical mechanics, objects exist in a specific place and time. In quantum mechanics, objects instead exist in a haze of probability. They have a certain chance of being at point A, another chance of being at point B.

Quantum physics states that the study of the universe and the study of consciousness are inseparably linked. Quantum physics is shattering the idea of there being an objectively existing world. Ironically, physics was long considered the most objective of the sciences, in pursuing the quest of understanding the nature of the universe, and quantum physics dispels the existence of a material objective universe. Quantum theory says that the observer, the observed, and the observation act are inseparable. You and I cause the shape of things. The mind changes subatomic particles to form your reality, which only exists in the observer's mind. Quantum physics is a threat to the underlying metaphysical assumptions of scientific materialism or objective reality separate from the observer.

Quantum theory causes you to question whether you are discovering reality or creating reality. Material or object reality is now an idea in your mind. What you call objective reality is simply an interpretation of data, whose meaning is agreed upon by most people and is called consensus reality. Reality is simply a theory and an internalized mental model of looking at the universe, instead of absolutely true knowledge of life's ultimate reality. You are participating in the creation of your experience in this world. You are dreaming up the genesis of the universe.

Without you observing the universe, it does not exist. Maybe you and I do not exist unless someone observes us! Quantum theory says that all creation is recreating itself continually, as you and I are dreaming it up. Viatko Vedral, Professor of Quantum Information Theory at Oxford, states that everything in the universe (including galaxies, planets, stars, and all matter) comprises the circuitry of a vast motherboard—all the information of the universe consisting of data bits. The universe is the result of a gigantic quantum computer.

Quantum theory says there is no objective reality without an observer. The act of observation is the very act that turns subatomic particles into reality. This belief significantly alters Descartes' famous statement, "I think, therefore I am," as quantum physics says, "I choose to be what I am."

If you and I create reality ourselves, you would think that we would make the world a more comforting and utopian-like place. There would be no sickness, war, or death. Therefore, we are dreaming up our reality very poorly! Maybe this book should be about training your mind to see a better reality versus an ultimate reality, which is factual and objective.

Quantum physics does not get humankind any closer to ultimate reality. What about other scientific models of reality? The Wavefunction-as-Reality model is famous and loved by science-fiction buffs. In the 1950s, Hugh Everett proposed the existence of multi-universes or parallel universes. The theory of many worlds believes that wavefunction governs reality's production so dramatically, that whenever a quantum measurement is made, the universe splits into parallel copies. David Kellogg Lewis proposed model realism—that all possible worlds are as real as the actual world. The actual world is just one of an infinite number of possible worlds, with some closer to the actual world and others more remote. These views are great for the science-fiction crowd, but they do not explain ultimate reality.

Another theory of reality is the brain-in-a-vat scenario. Everything you and I experience in the world is through our five senses. A sophisticated computer is manipulating our brains through the neural pathways to give us our perceptions. The popular Matrix series is an example of this theory. If we look further into other versions of computer-generated realities, there are computer-generated virtual reality video games. Technology is becoming so advanced that we can create a computer-generated virtual world. In the future, reality will be more challenging to realize. With the nature of human beings as they are, many people may live continually in a virtual world that they create.

Most people believe there is an objective reality, in which we all live with facts and physical laws that are present and not a matter of opinion. As you can see from the previous discussions, many people argue that there is no such thing as objective reality—everything is subjective or relative. Objective reality means that *something exists independent of the mind.* Subjective reality implies that *reality is in the eye of the observer.* Other words you may have heard that are similar are realism and anti-realism. Realism is the belief that there is a reality independent of any personal beliefs or perceptions. Anti-realism believes that objects of perception occur in the mind. Reality is a mental construct.

> It may come as a severe shock if you haven't given much thought to this subject before, but our precious, cast-in-stone, objective beliefs are often totally in contrast to any reality. Or, more accurately, they are our perception of reality, rather than reality itself.
>
> — Robert White

Scientists have been trying to determine the origin of the universe and reality. Most scientists agree that there was a big bang or sudden emergence of the universe, but they cannot explain how matter or energy miraculously formed from nothing. How did matter exist in a void for a universe to begin? What is the genesis causing matter to interact with other matter? People have been pondering these questions since the time of Aristotle to Morpheus, offering Neo the red or blue pill in the Matrix. The thought that we might not know or perceive reality has troubled and tantalized humans forever. This pursuit of reality matters, because it underpins everything we think about, know, believe, hope for, and dream.

Only someone or something that existed before there was matter, could create objective material from nothing and design it in such an intricate and marvelous manner. A divine, omnipotent designer and creator is the only One who could accomplish the universe's sudden appearance. God spoke the universe into existence—and Jesus Christ is the center of God's creation.

Colossians 1:15-20 NLT

Christ is the visible image of the invisible God.
He existed before anything was created and is supreme
over all creation,

for through him God created everything
in the heavenly realms and on earth.
He made the things we can see
and the things we can't see—
such as thrones, kingdoms, rulers, and authorities in the
unseen world.
Everything was created through him and for him.

He existed before anything else,
and he holds all creation together.

Christ is also head of the church,
which is his body.
He is the beginning,
supreme over all who rise from the dead.
So he is first in everything.

For God in his fullness
was pleased to live in Christ,

and through him God reconciled
everything to himself.
He made peace with everything in heaven and on earth
by means of Christ's blood on the cross.

Christians disagree on politics, church government, moral questions (such as abortion and sex), church doctrine, and nearly everything under the Sun. Still, a unity remains for almost all Christians, around God's core principles and the world God created. Ultimate reality is based on God as the sole, absolute power, metaphysical source, and sustainer of the universe seen and unseen. God is the heart of ultimate reality. An all-powerful God sustains, governs, controls, connects, and is integral to all creation. Only a nihilist can believe that there is no source or purpose to life and reality. If God is the only logical etiology of the universe's creation, God is the ultimate reality source. Whatever is deemed real is secondary or dependent on God's reality. It is God who gives weight to reality.

God created the laws of physics that hold the universe together. His laws of physics have remained stable and dependable since creation. There is no disorder or arbitrariness in this world. All the natural laws and moral laws were placed in creation by God. This objective world exists, not by itself, but through the will of God. It is what God willed it to be. Ultimate reality is God's idea and the realization of His will. Therefore, reality comes only from God's thoughts and will.

A worldview is the outward representation of your paradigm. It provides you with a guideline on living your life. God is being removed from the worldview of people in America. Culture and society will gradually fall into chaos from this change. If you noticed through the discussion of worldviews, they could be divided into three basic possible categories. I heard this on the radio broadcast of <u>Just Thinking</u> by the late Ravi Zacharias.

First, there is the worldview that there is only spirit or god. Everyone is a god or part of a universal god. Existence is through the spirit, and there is no physical world.

Second, there is the world view that there is only the physical universe. Everything is composed of atoms, particles, and follows the laws of physics. You and I are a bunch of DNA. There is the worldview that there is spiritual and physical existence.

Third, God created the physical world. He made man in His image with a spirit and soul housed in a physical body. All world views fall into these three categories—and you can evaluate the validity beginning with these three categories.

Real hope is grounded in reality, and the ultimate truth of reality is that we are loved by a busy God – one who never stops working in us.

— Michael Kelly

The Christian worldview answers all the questions of origin, meaning, morality, and destiny. It is truthful, factual, and logical. God is the Creator of the universe and humankind. The purpose of our lives is to serve and worship God. The moral laws of the world are given to us by God. Our final destination is to live in heaven with God, the Holy Spirit, and Jesus.

For Christians ultimate reality is and can only be a personal, sovereign, holy, and loving God. But even some Christians, under extra-biblical and even anti-Christian cultural influences, read the Bible as pointing to something

not ultimate, such as material wealth, health, happiness,
power, etc.

— Roger E. Olsen

Ultimate reality does exist. Sometimes your perceptions or understanding about the world may not match true reality. There are also illusions in the physical world that may confuse your observation ability. You may become blind to the reality that is right in front of you.

Magicians rely on techniques of illusion to perform their tricks. There are also illusions in nature. Context, color, texture, shadows, and other characteristics can alter what you see and are an integral part of perception. Another major obstacle to achieving the perfect perception of reality is *paradigm restriction*. Your paradigm keeps you from seeing the world as it exists. You need to train yourself to be observant and have an open mind. Perceptions are moods and emotionally dependent. You need to be aware of your state of mind during any observations.

Human beings use their minds to interpret reality and
sort the truth from the false. A physical, compromised,
inherent bias, and lack of awareness can lead a person
into misconstruing reality, and confusing what is true and
false. A person living a deluded life of sins and poverty
must reexamine their life and develop a proper and
sustainable life plan.

— Kilroy J. Oldster

The world has always been round, but it was believed to be flat for thousands of years. Was it ever flat? Absolutely not! Did people live like it was flat? Absolutely! People lived in fear who sailed the seas, as they were afraid they would fall off the Earth into a den of sea monsters. Without knowing the ultimate reality of life and having a Christian worldview, people live with fear, anxiety, stress, and worry. All the philosophers, scientists, and theorists keep searching for the answers to the reality of life. They keep beginning their search without including the world's Creator. Therefore, they will never find the true answer. Most people of the secular world live in fear of not knowing reality and their destiny. They fear death, because death is the end. Ultimate reality reveals that death is a transition from life to life and not life to death. Jesus spoke these words to Martha.

John 11:25 NLT

Jesus said to her, "I am the resurrection and the life. The one who believes in me will live, even though they die, and whoever lives by believing in me will never die. Do you believe this?

Ultimate reality is the highest, deepest, eternal, unchangeable source and ground of everything we see, touch, and experience with our five senses. It's that which gives being and meaning to everything finite, mortal, changeable. It's also that toward which we creatures look and live -whether we know it or not- our telos; goal and purpose.

— Roger E. Olsen

The moment you believe in Jesus as your Lord and Savior, you begin your journey to pure vision, perfect perception, and ultimate reality. The veil or fog over your eyes is lifted and you begin your eternal life. Once things in life were hazy and cloudy, like looking into a distorted mirror. It was difficult seeing through the fog of lies, propagated by Satan and the secular world. Now you can gain clarity by developing pure spiritual vision and perfect perception, which leads to ultimate reality. Ultimate reality is a beautiful thing. It is given to us by God and is a gift of His grace and love!

Epilogue

The Eye is the Window
to Your Soul and Spirit

Seeing 20/20 does not mean you have perfect vision

— James E. Croley III, M.D.

This book came about because the Holy Spirit instilled the thought in my mind—nearly all sin initially enters through your vision. After I finished the book, another idea came to me—I needed to change the book's title. Not only does sin enter the soul through the eyes, but America has been blinded by the propaganda blasting its mind through its eyes.

Before flat screens, it took some effort to find sinful things with your eyes. You could trust what you saw on a flat screen. You had to travel somewhere, buy magazines, books, or go somewhere to find sin. Now, all you have to do is pull out your smartphone and google anything you want to view. Everyone needs to be very careful about what they spend time viewing or watching. The eye is the window to your soul and spirit.

The most effective way of communicating with people is through images. The language of pictures is universal. Today

200

we are living in a world of continuous propaganda and lies. You and I are spending hours a day on a variety of flat screens. The Millennials and Zoomers have always grown up with flat screens by their side. Unfortunately, they have been manipulated by what they are viewing each day. Their belief system is entirely different from previous generations. Images, videos, and movies touch the emotions much more profoundly and personally than books or other communication forms. When you see pain on a flat screen, you feel the pain as well. If you see something sad or some form of injustice, it directly affects your heart.

The problem with flat screens is that what is being presented may not be true. This book is about training yourself toward better vision and perception. This training is more important for parents and children. Grandparents can learn this, also. They can be helpful with teaching or inspiring their children and grandchildren. We are living in a fog of lies and propaganda. How can you protect yourself and your family?

Flat screens and social media are powerful tools. They are extremely useful, when used correctly. The key is controlling what you are watching, versus flat screens controlling you. There is a ferocious battle going on, to control your mind with forces seen and unseen!

Ephesians 6:10-18 NLT

A final word: Be strong in the Lord and in his mighty power. Put on all of God's armor so that you will be able to stand firm against all strategies of the devil. For we are not fighting against flesh-and-blood enemies, but against evil rulers and authorities of the unseen world, against mighty powers in this dark world, and against evil spirits in the heavenly places. Therefore, put on every piece of God's armor so you will be able to resist the enemy in the time of evil. Then after the battle you will still be standing firm. Stand your ground, putting on the belt of truth and the body armor of God's righteousness. For shoes, put on the peace that comes from the Good News so that you will be fully prepared. In addition to all of these, hold up the shield of faith to stop the fiery arrows of the devil. Put on salvation as your helmet, and take the sword of the Spirit, which is the Word of God.

The secular world is ruthlessly pressing its agenda forward twenty-four hours a day. It is relentless and intense. They do not follow the rules of decency or ethics. They are willing to do anything, if it promotes their agenda. If you are old enough, you will remember that the TV turned off at eleven o'clock at night. The national anthem played and the TV screen turned to snow. All three TV channels went off at the same time! There was a break from flat screen viewing.

It is time to put everyone on a media or flat screen diet. Nearly eighty-five percent of people get their news on the internet. Many people realize that national news outlets have lost all integrity. The internet, Big Tech, news outlets, and social media are unreliable. Millennials get their news and politics from Twitter, Facebook, and others forms of social media. Everyone should know how misleading those sources are today, but, unfortunately, that is not the case.

At the time of writing this book, the Coronavirus was spreading worldwide for the past year. Social distancing and isolation are adding to the stress, uncertainty, fear, and anxiety. People are more disconnected than they have ever been. Everyone is glued to their flat screen during this time of isolation. The breakdown of culture and society has been ramped up to a torrid pace. Seventy-five percent of young people have had complaints about a mental disorder during this time of isolation. Mary Eberstadt, in her book, <u>How the West Really Lost God</u>, says, *The fortunes of religion rise and fall with the state of the family.*

Flat screens and the educational system have taken over the development of our children. Secularism is educating our children. They are teaching naturalism, materialism, and truths or facts are relative. We are in the middle of a post-truth worldview. Militant secularism states that all faith claims are merely subjective beliefs. Children are drowning and failing, while their parents are sitting there addicted to their flat screens! What can you do about it? Train your vision and develop improved perception skills. You need to commit to connecting yourself to the ultimate reality of life, God.

Visual temptations are everywhere, with evil influences continually pushing you and me toward sin. If you do not form a game plan to control these influences, you will unwittingly drift downstream towards destruction. You must equip yourself with the skills to overcome the onslaught of visual stimulation in today's world. You need control how flat screens influence you and your family's lives. You need to be very careful and not think that the temptation is only on a flat screen—that you can handle what you see watching them. Please do not deceive yourself. A quick view, just a little time on the internet, a little time playing an online game—these are just a few baby steps, leading to a slippery slope toward addiction to your flat screen devices. Consequently, you are always ultimately responsible for your sins.

It is a sinful and carnal perspective that believes eliminating sin from your life will leave a void in your life—that life will be dull and boring. You will not have any fun or joy in life. The only true void in someone's life is the void placed in you by God—and only He can fill it. The fundamental heart problem exists in your soul. The only solution is to fill your soul with the Holy Spirit.

Big tech, mass media, the secular world, and social media are determined to change your way of thinking and control your life. They want God removed from all aspects of life. But like it says in Romans 12:2, don't copy the behavior and customs of this world, but let God transform you into a new person by changing the way you think. You need to see through the lies and propaganda promoted by them. Unfortunately, anything you see on TV or social media is most likely presented for a reason—and is not reliable or factually correct. If there is an important topic you want information about, do your own research.

Open your mind to new possibilities and never stop learning. You should read the Bible every day, as it is full of educational recommendations. There are many resources of a religious nature available in books, the internet, TV, and apps. It is essential to develop a God-centered paradigm or perspective to bolster your connection with God. You should always base your beliefs on God's Word. Occasionally stop and take in a scenic view of this world God has created. Spend time observing the beauty, splendor, and fantastic design of the world. This time will help you develop a deeper and more meaningful understanding of God's power and majesty.

The things available on flat screens are appalling. The culture and society in America are rapidly deteriorating. Without God and the family, we are doomed. Just like other countries in the past, we will crumble from within in America! The focus of your eyes needs to be spiritually based. You can use art as a means of developing your perception skills. Have fun observing people and their body language. You should take time every day and pay attention to your observation skills. You will notice that your vision and observation abilities improve with time.

You need to be careful about your use of flat screens. Here are some guidelines.

- Routinely turn off your phone or flat screens to give yourself a break.
- Disable your flat screen notifications, so that you are not always anticipating a notice.
- Monitor your use of flat screens.
- If you are constantly checking your smartphone, limit the number of times you check it.
- Try to limit some of your social media apps.
- Spend more time offline with friends. Meet friends for lunch or after work.
- Set aside time each week to meet face-to-face with others.
- Develop a hobby or join a club.
- Use your flat screens in an intelligent and useful manner.

You need to be an active parent in the education of your young ones. You should make your voice known about what the educational system is teaching. Set up new rules for raising your children and grandchildren. Go to the PTA meetings and school board meetings and monitor their actions.

Limit screen time:

- Spend time each day with personal interaction with your children and with others.
- Monitor all flat screen activity of your children and keep track of what they are watching.
- Inform your kids about the dangers of social media.
- Teach your kids about social media as not being an accurate representation of people's real lives.
- Encourage discussions with your children about what they are watching alone and with you.
- Turn off all flat screens during meals.
- Turn off all flat screen devices at least one hour before bed to improve sleep patterns.
- Do not let a flat screen be in front of your children more than you are.
- Put filters on all flat screen devices.
- Find a church home and find playmates for your kids.
- Go to websites with the right set of morals and values to interact in a positive manner, such as PragerU.com.
- Control what apps are on all flat screens.

Add **religious apps** for your use and your kids' use. Here is a list of a few apps: Bible for kids, Bible ABCs for kids, Jesus loves me, God for kids, Sunscool, Bible color, Noah's Elephant in the Room, David versus Goliath, and Noah's Bible Memory Game.

Video Games:

The Bible Game, Dance Praise 2: The Remix, King of Kings: The Early Years, Bible Builder, Exodus, and Left Behind: Eternal Forces are a few choices.

Society in America is spiraling rapidly downward as the addiction to flat screens has a tight vice grip on the minds of Americans. Just like the Roman Empire and others before, America is crumbling. America was once a country that believed in God and family but is turning away from God, and the family is disintegrating. You need to teach your children and grandchildren about pure vision, perfect perception, and ultimate reality. You should teach them how to think and study things in a rational, logical, and inquisitive manner. They should not accept what they see on flat screens at face value but look further into the reasons behind what is propagated on the flat screens they are glued to watching.

Ephesians 4:14-16 NLT

Then we will no longer be immature like children. We won't be tossed and blown about by every wind of new teaching. We will not be influenced when people try to trick us with lies so clever they sound like the truth. Instead, we will speak the truth in love, growing in every way more and more like Christ, who is head of the body, the church. He makes the whole body fit together perfectly. As each part does its own special work, it helps the other parts grow, so that the whole body is healthy and growing and full of love.

Look what Paul says about humankind in the Roman Empire. It eerily looks like the culture in America today.

Romans 1:18-32 NIV

The wrath of God is being revealed from heaven against all the godlessness and wickedness of people, who suppress the truth by their wickedness, since what may be known about God is plain to them, because God has made it plain to them. For since the creation of the world God's invisible qualities—his eternal power and divine nature—have been clearly seen, being understood from what has been made, so that people are without excuse.

For although they knew God, they neither glorified him as God nor gave thanks to him, but their thinking became futile and their foolish hearts were darkened. Although they claimed to be wise, they became fools and exchanged the glory of the immortal God for images made to look like a mortal human being and birds and animals and reptiles.

Therefore God gave them over in their sinful desires of their hearts to sexual impurity for the degrading of their bodies with one another. They exchanged the truth about God for a lie, and worshiped and served created things rather than the Creator—who is forever praised. Amen.

Because of this, God gave them over to shameful lusts, Even their women exchanged natural sexual relations for unnatural ones. In the same way the men also abandoned natural relations with women and were inflamed with lust for one another. Men committed shameful acts with other men, and received in themselves the due penalty for their error.

Furthermore, just as they did not think it worthwhile to retain the knowledge of God, so God gave them over to a depraved mind, so that they do what ought not to be done. They have become filled with every kind of wickedness, evil, greed, and depravity. They are full of envy, murder, strife, deceit, and malice. They are gossips, slanderers, God-haters, insolent, arrogant, and boastful; they invent ways of doing evil; they disobey their parents; they have no understanding, no fidelity, no love, no mercy. Although they know God's righteous decree that those who do such things deserve death, they not only continue to do these things but also approve of those who practice them.

Humanity keeps making the same mistakes over and over. America has been blinded and is unaware of its circumstances. Today's difference is that the enemy has more and more potent weapons than in the past to control the masses. The power of addiction to the technology of flat screens is extremely powerful!

I hope this book has inspired you to seek God and turn away from sin. You are in charge of your vision and control what goes into your eyes—because what goes in will eventually control you. Your brain is like a computer—garbage in, garbage out. Through the Holy Spirit's strength, strive to develop pure vision and see the world with spiritual eyes or through a God-centered paradigm. This will help you obtain perfect perception through the power of the Holy Spirit. Pure vision and perfect perception lead to ultimate reality—and God is the source of all things.

Remember the famous line of Darth Vader, when he says this about Luke Skywalker—*the force is strong with this one.* How great would it be that a family member, a friend, or a stranger said this about you? The Holy Spirit is strong with this one!

Pure vision, perfect perception, and ultimate reality is the pathway to living a life with God.

The pathway to a life in Christ does exist.

May you have the vision and perception to see it,

the faith to get on it, and the perseverance to stay on it.

— James E. Croley III, M.D.

Bibliography

Chapter 1:

Page 3, Mere Christianity by C.S Lewis Reading literature allows us to see with different eyes.

Page 9, Journal Cognition article, Eyes are Where the Soul is Located by Christina Starmans and Paul Bloom at Yale University at Mind and Development Lab

Chapter 3:

Page 27, The Structure of Scientific Revolutions by Thomas Samuel Kuhn "all people, scientists see what they expect to see"

Page 28, Paradigms—The Business of Discovering the Future by Joel Barker "Five components of strategic exploration and anticipation

Page 41, The Rorschach Test developed by Swiss psychiatrist Herman Rorschach in 1921. The inkblot test measures various unconscious components of a subject's personality.

Chapter 4:

Page 48, Institutes of the Christian Religion by John Calvin. Scripture is like a pair of spectacles that enables you to see the world you live in the proper context.

Chapter 5:

Page 68,   Dopamine Fasting by Dr. Cameron Sepath, clinical professor of psychiatry at the University of California, San Francisco.

Page 70,   JAMA Pediatrics 2020 article "Association Between Screen-Based media Use and Brain White Matter Integrity in Preschool-Aged Children" by JS Hutton, J Dudley, T Horowitz-Kraus, and T DeWitt

Page 71, The Arrival of the Train by Lumiere Brothers. First commercially shown movie in 1896.

Chapter 6:

Page 96, Generations by Neil Howe and William Strauss coined the term Millennials.

Page 103, Minneapolis Star Tribune (http://www.startribune.com/as-minnesota-churches-close-a-way-of-life-fades/486037461/) on July 8, 2018, about the failing churches in Minnesota.

Page 103, Scot Thumma, director of the Hartford Institute for Religion Research (http://hirr.hartsem.edu/), predicts, "In the next twenty years, you will have half as many open congregations as now."

Page 103, Religion News Service (https://religionnews.com/2018/06/26/why-millennials-are-really-leaving-religion-its-not-just-politics-folks). The Southern Baptists have lost more than one million members in the last decade.

Page 103, University of Kentucky study in 2017 (https://psyarxiv.com/edzda) to get an accurate answer about the prevalence of atheists in America.

Page 104, Danbury Baptists Association wrote a letter to President-elect Thomas Jefferson in 1801, asking his opinion on a matter of Church and State.

Page 106, Coming Apart: The State of White America 1960-2010 by Charles Murray. Class stratification of White America.

Page 108, A practical Guide to Culture/ Helping the Next Generation Navigate Today's World by John Stonestreet and Brett Kunkle. Discusses culture and its influence on today's young people.

Page 108, Christianity and Culture by T.S. Eliot. This book contributes to the understanding of the nature of Culture and Christianity.

Page 114, Saving Truth / Finding Meaning and Clarity in a Post-Truth World. The book talks about the loss of truth and its effect on culture and society today.

Page 116, Margin: How to Create the Emotional, Physical, Financial, and Time Reserves You Need by Richard A, Swenson M.D. Margin is "the space that once existed between ourselves and our limits".

Chapter 7:

Page 119, Study titled Frequency and the Conference of Referential Validity by Lynn Hasher and David Goldstein Temple University and Thomas Toppino at Villanova University. The study researched The Illusionary Effect as a principle of psychology related to the fact that when something is repeated enough times, people will believe it's true even if it is untrue.

Page 120, Knowledge Does Not Protect Against Illusionary Truth in the Journal of Experimental Psychology by Lisa K. Kazio, Nadia M. Brasier, Keith Payne, and Elizabeth Marsh. The Illusionary Truth Effect could change a person's belief of the truth through false repetition of a false statement.

Page 126, Persuasive Technology by Stanford researcher B.J. Fogg is known as the father of persuasive technology. He referred to this field of study as captology or CAPT. Using flat screen technology to change the way you live your life and shape the way you believe.

Page 145, Bias: A CBS Insider Exposes How Media Distort the News by Bernard Goldberg in 2001. A book about how CBS distorts the news to fit their agenda.

Chapter 8:

Page 158, Visual Intelligence/ Perception, Image, and Manipulation in Visual Communication by Ann Marie Seward Barry.

Page 159, Visual Intelligence/ Sharpen Your Perception, Change Your Life by Amy E. Herman.

Page 159, Visual Literacy is the ability to understand and use images including the ability to think, learn, and express oneself in terms of images by Braden and Hortin.

Page 161, A Whack on the Side of the Head by chaos theorist Roger vonOech. Everyone believes theirs is the right answer mentally. But if you think there is only one right answer, you will stop looking as soon as you find one.

CPSIA information can be obtained
at www.ICGtesting.com
Printed in the USA
LVHW051021310122
709513LV00007B/17